families on Mission

Ideas for Teaching Your Preschooler to Love, Share, and Care

ANGIE QUANTRELL

wMu

Birmingham, Alabama

Woman's Missionary Union, SBC
P. O. Box 830010
Birmingham, AL 35283-0010

For more information, visit our Web site at www.wmu.com or call 1-800-968-7301.

Dewey Decimal Classification: 248.82
Subject Heading: FAMILY—RELIGIOUS LIFE
                 FAMILY LIFE
                 CHILDREN—FAMILY LIFE

Design by Janell E. Young

ISBN-10: 1-56309-991-8
ISBN-13: 978-1-56309-991-5
W058105•0905•5M1

Dedication

This book is dedicated to Jesus Christ, my All-in-all and my Resource, Who planned for and loves families and preschoolers! He is the Perfect One, and seeks to draw each of us, regardless of age, size, color, or condition, closer to Him.

"Now may the God of hope fill you with all joy and peace in believing, that you may abound in hope by the power of the Holy Spirit" (Rom. 15:13 NKJV).

"And whatever you do, do it heartily, as to the Lord and not to men, knowing that from the Lord you will receive the reward of the inheritance; for you serve the Lord Christ" (Col. 3:23–24 NJKV).

Contents

Introduction

About Families and Preschoolers

Welcome! You are members of a wild, crazy, fast-paced, and wonderful life—parents and guardians of preschoolers! This is a special stage in your life—a life you will revel in one moment, and despair in the next! Raising preschoolers is not a task for the fainthearted!

When my teenagers were preschoolers (can it be that time has gone so fast?), I loved the cute smiles, the funny things they said and did, the way they grew and changed overnight, and the absolute love shared between us. On the other hand, I constantly lacked sleep; someone was always sick; the house was never clean; and meals and laundry were unending. But through it all, I knew that God had a plan for me, a special task to care for and raise my preschoolers to know Him. I was blessed to stay at home and care for my preschoolers. My husband and I took very seriously the responsibility of raising our children in the ways of the Lord.

In His infinite wisdom, God created the family. The family is His plan for having babies, loving preschoolers, teaching children, and raising adults who are committed, responsible, serving Christians. *God created parents to be the first and most important teachers in a child's life!* Parents have the most influence over members in their family—beginning at birth and continuing through adulthood.

Families are the perfect setting for teaching how to get along, how to love, how to forgive, how to share, and how to care for others. It is a wonderful place to learn how to communicate and share feelings and ideas with others. It is even the best place to experience disagreements and arguments, learn to deal with disharmony, and restore harmony. A family filled with love for each other is a safe haven from the pressures and influences of the outside world. God created family to be a nurturing environment for passing on Christian values, morals, and habits—climate control over the outside influences of world standards and views. What a wonderful plan God has put into place!

You are your child's best teacher! Living as a committed, serving Christian is a powerful role model for your children. It seems there is never enough time or energy, but lavish both on your family. The preschool years are important in laying the foundations of a Christian lifestyle. Preschoolers are sponges; they soak in what they see, hear, and do! When your preschooler observes you praying for others; giving yourself, your time, and your resources to help others; and sharing the love and story of Jesus, he will see and learn from your examples.

An important part of a Christian walk is service. All Christians are called to serve one another and tell about God's plan of salvation. All believers are called to pour out energy, time, resources, and self to spread the message of Jesus. Begin at home, and invest yourself in your preschooler. Love, care for, and teach your preschooler. Pour your heart and soul into raising them in a Christian home—God's purpose for your family, an eternal investment.

Sound like an insurmountable task? Don't despair! Help is available. God's plan all along was to give us Jesus, the Holy Spirit, and the Holy Bible. He also gave us each other—our friends and family, our church, and our extended Christian family. Together, we can share ideas, help and care for each other, work together, give to each other, and pray for and love each other. Families helping families is part of God's plan.

What is missions?

Missions is service. Missions is a lifestyle of serving Jesus and others. It is a commitment to following what the Bible instructs us to do as we raise our families in a Christian home. Missions is anything we do to tell about Jesus, serve others, help others, care for and love others, and live a Christian lifestyle. Each Christian is called to serve, to live a life of significance in service for God and to others whom He loves. Every believer is a missionary, someone who loves and tells others about Jesus. Believers must disciple others—show and teach people how to live a godly life. We are to walk with others, share the love of Jesus, help the best we can, and serve by following the example given by Jesus in the Bible.

Service to others, missions, is a lifestyle. It is a daily choice to look beyond ourselves and our family needs and schedules, and see and take opportunities for serving others. Because of the age of preschoolers, choices in serving others (missions involvement) will be simple. Missions activities will be geared toward the ability of preschoolers to help and feel important in the process. Preschoolers need to see parents and family members concerned and involved in service to others. Preschoolers thrive on participation. They need simple explanations to build understanding. Watching, learning, and participating will help young family members grow spiritually, and will start them on the road toward a lifestyle of service.

Simply put: Missions is learning about Jesus, doing what He did for others, and telling others about Him.

What is a missionary?

What do you think of when you hear the word *missionary*? Many people think a missionary is a person who tells about Jesus in an international location. Some think only missionaries have to tell about Jesus. The truth is that all who believe in Jesus are missionaries! In the Bible, all Christians are commanded to go and tell about Jesus (Matt. 28:19–20). Go, serve, and tell. But don't be frightened! Not all going is long-distance. Going can be as close as walking out your front door and talking to a neighbor. Going can be playing with other families at a local park. Going sometimes means serving in a distant country, or it could mean traveling to a nearby city, county, or state to tell about Jesus.

All people who serve Jesus are missionaries. All people who do missions are serving Jesus and others. Even though it seems you are constantly on the go, and your world is upside down with the demands of caring for your preschooler, remember that God has placed you in His hand. He will care for you. Now is the time to enjoy your family, and begin to instill in your child the love of and service to the Lord.

How to Use This Book

This book is divided into chapters about different ways and places to serve others. Each chapter contains a short explanation about the topic, and then gives ideas for activities and projects that relate to that topic. A list of needed materials and ideas of things to say to preschoolers is included with the activities. Read each chapter introduction for an understanding of what each topic is and why it is important for a lifestyle of serving others.

Several projects and activities revolve around the Bible. Keep your family Bible in an easy-to-use location. Bible verses and Bible thoughts are listed in each chapter. These are the biblical basis of why each topic is important in serving others (being on mission). Bible thoughts are taken from the Bible. These phrases are simplified Bible verses that are easy for preschoolers to understand and memorize. Each Bible thought reflects an important Bible concept or idea. Work together to locate and read the Bible thoughts and verses. This will show the importance of reading and knowing about the Bible.

Talk with your family about serving others—being on a mission for God. Explain why it is important to do what you are going to do. Every preschooler is different. Preschoolers have short attention spans, develop at their own pace, and have different interests. Choose activities or projects that will work for your family. Adapt each activity to your family situation, taking into account where you live, the supplies you have, your work schedule and finances, and the church you attend. Simplify or substitute materials to fit your family.

This book is a guide to help your family experience ways to serve others. Doing missions (serving others) combines family time, Christian education, service to others, and participation in Jesus' plan for your lives. Go for it! Enjoy!

1

Loving

Read More About It: John 3:16; Romans 12:9–13; 1 Corinthians 13:1–7,13; 1 Corinthians 16:13–14
Bible Thoughts for Preschoolers
Jesus loves you (see John 15:12).
Love one another (see 1 John 4:7).

What is loving?

Love, cherish, adore, beloved—all of these words speak of deep affection. To love is to have deep affection and intense feelings for another person. Loving is the way we express our love.

Think back to your wedding day, or the day that your child was born. You experienced feelings of love for that special person. Most parents of a newborn feel joy, protectiveness, and overwhelming love. It is amazing how we, as parents, fall deeply in love with our tiny, helpless, wrinkled babies! It is even more amazing to see how our love grows and matures as our babies grow and mature. We learn to love our little ones or our spouses through good times and bad times. Not because the loved one deserves it, or does things to please us. We love because we want to love, and we can't help it!

Loving is an expression of love to others. Love is shown through words and actions. Our family members will be able to tell that we love them by the way we talk, act, and treat them. First, we have to practice and teach loving at home. We need to love and cherish our family. Then, we need to reach out and love others outside of our family. Our world needs to see love, Jesus' love, in action. Loving others by what we do and say shows the world that we are Christians. Loving others draws them to Jesus and makes them want to know the love that we have.

Why is loving important?

First John 4:7–8 says that God *is* love. Love is a part of God's plan. Not only did He love us enough to create us, He gave us an example of perfect love in Jesus Christ. He sacrificed His only Son, Jesus, to show us how much He loved us. God's plan was for Jesus to become human, and show us how to love. With the Bible, God gave us a source of information about how to love. Our job, as parents and as believers in Christ, is to read and learn as much as we can about love. And then we need to love our family, and teach and show our preschoolers how to love.

God created us with the capacity and need for love. Many times the feelings of love are mingled with care, concern, adoration, enjoyment, pride, control, ownership, jealousy. . . . Look at today's society and it becomes evident that many feelings are mixed up in love. Worldly love is not the same as Christian love. God gave parents the job of teaching their families about the kind of love found in the Bible, godly love. That is why it is important for parents to learn about, practice, and teach their preschoolers what it means to love.

How can I teach my preschooler to love?

The best way to teach your preschooler to love is to show love to your preschooler! Simple, but important! Show your child how to express love. Teach how to say "I love you" or "I care for you."

Demonstrate physical signs of love such as giving a hug, a good-night kiss, snuggling, and holding hands on a walk. Talk about love, what it means, and appropriate ways to show love. Teach siblings to love, share, respect, and care for each other.

Take love outside of your home. Encourage your child to show loving actions, words, and attitudes toward others. Practice a loving lifestyle as you go about your daily lives. Teach by example. Let your child catch you acting like Jesus. Loving actions can take place at the supermarket, the library, the doctor's office, and the city park. Loving others can be as simple as holding the door open for another, or as involved as working together with your church to serve meals to the homeless. Be more like Jesus, and your child will want to be more like Jesus.

As a parent, you are the first and best teacher for your child! Create a loving atmosphere in your home. With your family, extend love to others whom you know. Teach loving by participation and experience.

Activities

Heart-Shaped Sandwiches

Ask your preschooler to help you make your favorite sandwiches. Use a metal heart-shaped cookie cutter to cut a heart out of the center of each sandwich. Separate the heart-shape from the rest of the sandwich and place it on a plate. Pray aloud, and say: Thank You, God, for giving me a wonderful child to love. Thank You for our food.

Tell your child that you love him. Eat heart sandwiches.

Jesus Loves You

During bathtime, sing "Jesus Loves You" with your child. Play in the warm bath water and sing the song. Continue singing the song as you wrap your child in a fuzzy towel, and snuggle close together. Say: Jesus loves you, and I love you!

Sing "Jesus Loves You" throughout your day. Babies and toddlers love to hear singing, even if they cannot sing along or do not know the words. Sing during diaper-changing time, while driving to the store, while washing dishes, or at the end of the day as you rock him to sleep. Your child will learn the song through the repetition of hearing it over and over. He will grow to understand that Jesus loves him.

Paint a Love Picture

Materials: watercolor paper, washable markers, paintbrush, cup of water

Let your child draw a self-portrait. Help her add details, such as fingers, hair, ears, and so on. Give her a paintbrush, and let her dip it in water, and paint over her drawing. The colors from the markers will run together, giving the appearance of a watercolor painting. Dry and display the painting on the refrigerator. Or ask your child to choose someone who needs a *love picture*, and help her deliver the picture. Say: I love you, and God loves you. Look at how wonderful He made you!

Welcome Wagon

Do you have new neighbors or a family that has recently moved into your area? Pull out the little red wagon, load up your preschooler, and take a walk to visit and welcome the newcomers. Introduce yourself and your child. Encourage your child to say hello. Ask the new family if they have any questions or needs that you can help with. Share basic information about your neighborhood, such as the location of the grocery store, post office, library, school, or park. Give your phone number, and extend the invitation to call if they need help with anything. Tell your child to wave good-bye as you walk home. Say: We showed love to our new neighbors. We welcomed them to our neighborhood!

Yarn Vase and Flowers

Materials: clean plastic or glass jar, multicolored yarn, glue, waxed paper, cut flowers

Place the jar on a piece of waxed paper. Let your preschooler spread glue over the outside of the jar. Beginning at the top of the jar, help your child wrap the yarn around the jar, putting the yarn on the jar in horizontal stripes. Keep the yarn close together so that the entire jar is covered. Clip the end of the yarn at the bottom of the jar. Dry.

Let your child fill the beautiful jar with cold water. Arrange cut flowers in the jar. Give the flower jar to someone that you both love. Share a hug and tell the person: "I love you!"

Chalk Messages

Purchase sidewalk chalk from a toy or variety store. Invite your preschooler to decorate your cement sidewalk or driveway. Draw fun and silly pictures. Show how to draw gigantic hearts. Print: *Jesus loves you!* and *Welcome!* in the hearts. Read the messages with your child. Say: When people read our chalk messages, they will hear that Jesus loves them. We are telling about Jesus' love for people.

Love Tag

Play this game with your family members, or invite neighborhood boys and girls to join in the fun. Choose one child to be "It" (an adult could be "It" the first time, to show how to play the game). Everyone runs from "It." "It" tries to catch others. If "It" tags another child, "It" must give a hug and say "I love you" or "Jesus loves you!" The child who was tagged is now "It." Continue playing love tag until all players have had a turn. Share a group hug when the game is finished. Say: Jesus loves you! I love you!

Photo Paperweight

Materials: large 4-to-6-inch smooth river rock, waxed paper, red acrylic paint, paintbrush, photo of your child or family, decoupage glue

Let your child wash the rock. Dry completely. Place the rock on a piece of waxed paper and ask your preschooler to paint it red. Make sure all surfaces are covered. After the paint dries, trim the photo to fit on the rock. Ask your preschooler to paint the rock with decoupage glue. Smooth the photo on the rock, and paint over the photo with the glue, sealing the photo to the rock. Dry, and add a second coat of decoupage glue. Deliver the paperweight to a grandparent or family friend. Let your child say "I love you!"

Visiting Pets

Visit a nursing home with your child and your family pet (dog, guinea pig, rabbit, or calm cat). Make arrangements prior to the visit by calling the nursing home.

On the day of the visit, help your preschooler groom the pet. Talk with your child about the visit, and prepare her for what she will see, hear, and smell. Say: People who live in nursing homes have to have extra help to do things. Some will be in a wheelchair; some will not be able to talk; some might smell funny; and some can't even get out of bed. But Jesus loves all of the people in the nursing home. He wants us to love them too!

Go to the nursing home. Let your child be in charge of the pet, but offer help and support. Keep the pet on a leash. Let your child share the pet. Encourage her to put the pet on a lap, or hold the pet up so residents can stroke the fur. Tell the pet's name, and visit with residents. Enjoy the time loving others.

After the trip, ask your child how she felt about the nursing home. Answer any questions she might have. If she enjoyed the trip, suggest that you make arrangements to go back again.

Hint: Take a photographer on the second trip. Take pictures of the nursing home residents, your child, and the pet. Develop the pictures and let your child give a copy to the residents. Tell residents that Jesus loves them.

Turn Down the Beds

Work together with your preschooler to treat family members like they are staying at a fancy hotel. Before bedtime, sneak into each room with your child. Turn down the covers, fluff the pillows, and place a small chocolate and red paper heart on each pillow. As family members prepare for bed, watch them light up with joy at the special treatment. With your preschooler, say, "We love you!"

Pray for the Feet of Others

Take a photo of each family member's feet. Develop the photos. Let your child cut red hearts from construction paper. Glue each photo in the center of a heart. Display the hearts in your home. Lead family members to pray for each other, their feet, and the places they walk daily. Pray for the people that family members see as they are walking. Pray that your family can be a loving example of Jesus to the people they see.

Talk about missionaries, people who serve others. Discuss missionaries who walk in different countries, taste different foods, learn a new language, live in a new house, go to a new school, and experience new customs. Pray with your family that missionaries will walk with the Lord through all of the new things they encounter.

FYI: All believers in Jesus Christ are missionaries! Everyone who loves Jesus serves others.

Bible Thoughts About Love

Sit with your preschooler. Hold the Bible on your lap, and look up the Bible thoughts for this chapter. Show your child where the verses are on the page. Point to the verses, and say the Bible thoughts. Say: The Bible tells us that Jesus loves you, and Jesus loves me! The Bible tells us to love one another. What are some ways we can show love to each other?

Let your child think of ways to show love. Choose one idea and follow his suggestion. Compliment him on his idea and how he shows love to others.

Ask your older preschooler to print the Bible thoughts on index cards. Tape them on the bathroom mirror. Read them every morning with your child. Choose one way to show love to another person each day.

Ideas for loving others: blow a kiss, make a bed, gather the laundry, cook a special meal, pick up toys, open a door, offer your chair, carry a grocery bag, pick up a dropped item, smile and say hello, let someone else go first, say a prayer.

Big Box Fun

Get a large cardboard box from a furniture store. Lay the box on its side, and make an opening. Lay pillows, a blanket, and a baby doll inside the box. Drape a blanket over the box. Crawl in and cuddle with your child. Allow your baby or toddler to crawl in and out of the box. Show loving actions as you play and pretend with your child, the box, and the baby doll. Follow the lead of your preschooler as she plays and makes up activities.

Cotton Ball Painting

Materials: large pieces of construction paper, marker, acrylic paint poured on paper plates, clothespins clipped onto cotton balls, apron

On the top of a piece of paper, print *Jesus loves* in small letters. Print your child's name in large letters across the middle of the paper. Show your child how to dip a clothespin paintbrush into the paint, and dab paint along the lines of his name. After he completes his name, give him a blank paper and let him make random designs. Display the paintings in his room. Say: This sign says Jesus loves Cody!

Idea: Let your child invite a friend to come over and paint a name poster. Let your preschooler tell his friend that Jesus loves him.

A Picnic with Friends

Enlist your preschooler to help you pack a picnic lunch. Pack enough food for two families. Pack simple family favorites like sandwiches, chips, cookies, juice boxes, cheese chunks, pickles, and other food items. Include paper plates, napkins, and hand wipes.

Invite another family to join yours for a picnic. Ask them to bring games and sports equipment for play time after the picnic. Meet at a park with jungle gym equipment or large grassy areas.

Before eating, lead both families in a short prayer. Thank God for love, friends, food, and fun. Socialize and play games that include all of the preschoolers and children that are present. Build a loving relationship with your new friends.

Birthday Love

Create a new family tradition of love! Visit a thrift store or discount store. Choose a special plate, cup, and hat (or crown) that is decorated with hearts. Use these items only on a family member's birthday.

On the day of your child's birthday, let her be the Person of the Day. Ask her to choose her favorite meals, including the design of her birthday cake or dessert. Allow her to wear the hat or crown, and eat meals using the special plate and cup. Show love and caring in how the special person is honored and enjoyed. Sing "Happy Birthday." To the same tune, sing:

We love you, we do!
We love you, we do!
We love you, our darling!
We love you, we do!

Heart Tree

Materials: red construction paper, scissors, glue, magazines, markers, hole punch, string, heart-shaped items (cookie cutter, toy, balloon, etc.), white Christmas lights strung on a tree in your yard or porch

Cut paper in half. Show your preschooler how to fold a piece in half, and cut a heart from the paper. Help hold scissors or draw a cutting line. Open the heart. Say: Look. You cut out a heart! A heart means love.

Let your child search a magazine for faces. Cut out a face, and let him glue the face on one side of the heart. After it dries, print: *Jesus loves you* on the back. Punch a hole in the top, add a string loop, and let your child hang the heart on the tree. Let family members make hearts, and hang them on the tree. Attach string loops to other heart-shaped items and hang them on the tree. Say: Jesus loves all people. He wants us to show love to others.

As guests visit your home, or neighbors walk past your house, give each a heart from the tree.

Tip: Decorate the tree each month with a seasonal decoration. Invite neighbors and their families to come and make ornaments, or deliver one to each neighbor after the month is over. Include a Bible thought or cheery saying on each ornament.

Ideas: snowflakes, flags, watermelons, flowers, eggs, kites, stars, pinecones, apples, pumpkins, and leaves.

What Do You Love?

Take a walk through your home or around your neighborhood. Ask your preschooler to point out things that she loves. Repeat what she says, and list the loved items. Say: Sammie loves the trees, the dog, the flowers, and our neighbor. What else do you love?

Spend time noticing the little things as you walk with your child. Draw attention to the people. Ask your child to tell who Jesus loves. Repeat what she says. Say: Jesus loves Sammie, Jesus loves Mommy, and Jesus loves all the people.

Heart Cookies

With your child, make heart-shaped sugar cookies. Break out the icing, butter knives, and sprinkles. Let your child spread icing and sprinkle decorations on the cookies. After the cookies are decorated, let your child choose one for each family member, and place them on a plate to keep for dessert or snacktime.

Let your child put several cookies on a paper plate. Cover the cookies with plastic wrap, and deliver the plate of cookies to someone who has been loving to your family: pastor, relative, teacher, or another favorite person. Tell how much you appreciate their loving actions.

Simon Says

Teach your child how to play "Simon says." Whatever Simon says ("Simon" is the appointed leader of the game), everyone else must copy. Take turns being "Simon." When it is your turn to be "Simon," instruct your child to do loving actions such as hug another person, kiss a hand, say thank you, or clap hands. Say: "Simon says" is a fun game where we copy the leader. Jesus wants us to copy Him, and love others.

Heart Cards

Materials: heart-shaped cookie cutters, acrylic paint poured on paper plates, marker, cardstock, apron

Show your child how to make cookie cutter prints on one side of the cardstock. Dip the cookie cutter in paint and stamp it on the cardstock. Use different sizes of cookie cutters and different colors of paint to make designs. Dry. Fold the cardstock in half. Print a Bible thought from this chapter inside the cards.

Let your child choose a card to send to someone she loves: a grandparent, an aunt or uncle, or a teacher. Print her message in the card; put it in an envelope; and let her put it in the mailbox. Say: You are thinking of another person. You are showing love. Jesus wants us to love others.

2
Sharing

Read More About It: Proverbs 11:25; Luke 6:38; 2 Corinthians 6:4; Hebrews 13:15–16
Bible Thoughts for Preschoolers
God is good to us (see Psalm 73:1).
God gives us things to enjoy (see 1 Tim. 6:17).

What is sharing?

Sharing is the ability to give a portion of belongings to another, so that each person has enough or an equal part. Sharing is being able to take turns with items, such as tools, toys, or gadgets. Sharing is unselfishness and generosity with material possessions. A person shows his ability to share by giving to others. Sharing is being able to look at others, see their needs, and give to meet the needs. Money, food, clothes, time, help, and material goods are just some of the things that can be shared. Love, forgiveness, tenderness, patience, wisdom, the gospel of Jesus—all of these are harder to see and measure, but all are just as important to share! Sharing is looking at what we have, seeing what someone else doesn't have, and finding a way to give to satisfy that need.

Learning to share is one of the most important goals in the life of a preschooler. As a parent, you spend considerable time showing and telling your child how to share with others. Sometimes, your child is very good at sharing things like colds, coughs, and the stomach flu! If your child spends time with a group of same-aged preschoolers, at day care, preschool, or Sunday School, you know that the teachers spend large amounts of time helping preschoolers learn to share.

Learning to share unreservedly, as God shared His only Son with us, takes a lifetime of lessons. Even as adults, we still sometimes have trouble sharing. Sharing is a wonderful family goal and habit!

Why is sharing important?

The Bible tells believers to take care of each other (see 1 Tim. 6:17-19). Taking care of others involves sharing. God blesses each person with certain gifts, such as a good job, a nice home, laughter, love, clothes, and food. God generously gives us the things we need, so we can turn around and give to others. He uses us to share His blessings with people less fortunate. We are an important part of God's plan: to share necessities with people who need them. Sharing the gospel, the story of the One Who is the giver of all gifts, Jesus, is a part of God's plan for us!

The Bible also tells believers to not focus on material things, but focus on Jesus, and eternal things (see Matt. 6:19–21). Sharing what we have and being generous with our belongings helps us see that what we have is not important. What we do with what we have is important! As we study the Bible, spend time in prayer, worship, and fellowship with other believers, we will grow closer to Christ. We will see the importance of sharing and taking care of others with what we have. We will learn to be more like Jesus.

How can I teach my preschooler to share?

Let's face it, sharing is a challenge for most preschoolers! The majority of preschoolers think only of themselves and what they want and need. That is a normal stage of development. Learning to share is a process that takes time, patience, and lots of practice.

As your preschooler has opportunities to interact with family members, children, and adults, she will experience many chances to share. Your child can share her toys, her food, her space, and her parents (especially if a new sibling comes along). She can also share affection, joy, kindness, concern for others, and love. Sometimes she will be able to share and enjoy herself in the process. Other times will not be as successful. Stay calm, and know that the next opportunity to share may be better.

Teach your preschooler to share by talking about sharing. As you share half of your sandwich or a drink of your milk, tell her that you enjoy sharing with her. If you notice her giving a toy to another child, say that you appreciate her sharing with others. As you play with your preschooler, share toys back and forth. Thank her for sharing the blocks or giving a car to a sibling. Meals are the perfect time to practice sharing. Eating snacks and food items with preschoolers is a meaningful way to emphasize sharing. Tell why sharing is important. Use opportunities during your day to share with your child, and offer the chance for your child to share with you. With practice and patience, sharing will soon become a family habit.

Activities

Waiting Room Read-aloud

Let your child select his favorite books about serving others to keep in your car. When going to a doctor or dentist appointment, ask your preschooler to carry the books in with him. Situate yourself in the child play area, and read the books aloud to your preschooler. Encourage him to invite others to listen to a story while they wait. Let him share his books with others. Engage waiting preschoolers and family members in conversation. Share in the daily lives of other parents who are raising preschoolers. Offer to pray for special needs that are mentioned as you visit.

Ask the receptionist if there is a need for toys or books for the waiting room. Offer to collect items and donate them to the office. Let your preschooler help you choose and deliver the needed books or toys. Say: We are sharing these toys and books with other boys and girls! Jesus is happy when we share.

Share Books About Jesus

Let your preschooler choose his favorite book about Jesus or missions (serving others for Jesus). Purchase a copy from a bookstore, catalog, or online. Take the book to your child's next doctor's appointment. Let him tell the doctor about the book and why it is his favorite. Let him give the book to the doctor, to place in the waiting room for other boys and girls to read. Say: You shared a book with your doctor. Other boys and girls can read the book that you shared.

Look for and read the book in the waiting room during your next visit. Remind him that he shared the book with others.

Hint: Call ahead to make sure office policy will allow your child to donate a book.

Your Favorite Candy, My Favorite Candy

When in a store, ask your preschooler to choose her favorite candy, while you choose your favorite also. Purchase the treats and share with each other. Tell about your feelings as you share candy. Say: It makes me happy when you share your favorite candy. It makes me glad to share my candy with you!

Beach Balls at the Beach

Inflate several beach balls. Use a permanent marker to write Bible thoughts from this book or the words Jesus Loves You on each ball.

With your preschooler, go to the beach or a park. Play catch, toss and roll, and have fun with the balls. Allow other preschoolers and children to join you. When you leave, give the Bible message beach balls to the preschoolers who were playing with them. To your child, say: We shared the beach balls. Now boys and girls can read about Jesus on their beach ball!

Cornucopia of Thanksgiving

Materials: cornucopia basket, toy fruits and vegetables, paper strips, tape, marker

Place the cornucopia basket on a coffee table. Let each family member choose a fruit or vegetable and say one thing he is thankful for. Print what he says on a strip of paper, help tape it to the chosen fruit or vegetable, and let him put it in the cornucopia basket. Continue with all of the fruits and vegetables.

As guests visit your home, let your child tell about the cornucopia of thankful thoughts. Say: You are sharing with your voice. You are telling others why you are thankful to God.

Tip: Find a cornucopia basket at a thrift or craft store.

Rock Collecting

Materials: plastic buckets, old toothbrushes, bar of soap, tub of water, apron

Preschoolers love to pick up and save rocks! Give each child in your family a sturdy, plastic bucket. Go for a walk along a beach, a dirt road, or a forest area. Tell your preschooler to look for pretty rocks and put them in her bucket. Take the rocks home.

Choose an area of your yard for a rock collection. Provide a tub of water, old toothbrushes, a bar of soap, and an apron. Let family members scrub the rocks clean with soap and a toothbrush. Together, share rocks to create a rock garden. Say: We are sharing rocks. When we share, everyone has plenty. We have enough rocks for our rock garden.

Caution: Collect rocks from an appropriate area. Avoid private or protected property.

Cookie Exchange

Invite another family from church or your neighborhood to join yours for a cookie exchange. Have each family work together to bake a batch of their favorite cookie recipe and bring it to your home. When baking, let your child do as much as possible, such as pour ingredients, mix dough, roll dough, and taste baked cookies!

When your friends arrive, let the preschoolers and children share the cookies with each other. Provide hot coffee and milk to drink while tasting cookies and visiting. Store extra cookies in large, self-sealing bags. Give each family a bag of cookies. After the guests have gone home, say: We shared today! We shared the work of making cookies, and we shared cookies with our friends! Jesus wants us to share our energy and our food with family and friends.

Kitchen Instruments

Place metal pots and pans, wooden spoons, and metal bowls on the floor. (Add a metal spoon if you are brave!) Sit on the floor with your baby or toddler and show how to use the kitchen utensils as instruments. Share the fun in making noise and music with your child. When other family members come in to see what the music is (they will call it noise), invite them to join the fun. Share the instruments.

Tip: Designate one floor-level cupboard for utensils that your child can play with as you prepare meals.

Zoo Animal Fun

With your preschooler, gather all the zoo animals from the toy box (or other animals). Use wooden blocks to build cages and pens. Share the zoo animals and play together. As you share animals, say: God made the animals. He shared them with us!

Take a trip to the zoo to look at the animals that God made. Share the trip with another family that has preschoolers.

Needed: Toys

Ask your church's preschool teacher what kinds of toys are needed for the Preschool Department (or a children's, women's, or homeless shelter). Make a list of needed items.

Talk to your preschooler about other people who don't have toys. Ask your child how he would feel if he didn't have toys. Shop at yard sales and thrift stores for toys on the list. Select toys that are in good condition. Let your child look for and give the money for toys. Clean and repair toys at home. Go together to deliver the toys. Say: You worked hard to find these toys. Thank you for sharing toys.

Share a Shake

Whip up an ice-cream shake. Combine ice cream, milk, and flavoring (chocolate or frozen fruit) in a blender. Blend until smooth. Pour into a glass. Add two straws. Share the milk shake with your preschooler. Say: I'm glad we can share this shake. Yummy!

Or, walk to a nearby ice-cream shop. Share an ice-cream cone, sundae, or shake with your child.

Share a Snuggle

Snuggle up on the couch with a warm, soft blanket. Talk about the day or interests of your child. Gently stroke your child's arms or hands, and smooth his hair back. Say: I love snuggling with you. Thanks for sharing this snuggle with me!

If your preschooler is a baby, snuggle and hum favorite melodies. Make eye contact, rub noses, and count his fingers. Share your love with your baby.

Easter Egg Giveaway

Materials: plastic eggs, heart-shaped candy, jelly beans, strips of paper printed with *Jesus Loves You* on one side and your church information on the other, baskets

Ask family members to stuff eggs with candy and a strip of paper. Help close the eggs and place them in baskets. On the Saturday before Easter, pass out eggs at a busy street corner or shopping area. Let your preschooler give away the eggs. Encourage family members to tell recipients "Happy Easter" or "Jesus Loves You." After the eggs have been given away, say: The Bible says to tell others about Jesus. Thank you for sharing!

Tip: Invite other families or Sunday School class members to work with your family on this project.

Plant a Garden

As a family, choose seeds or seedlings for favorite vegetables. Work together to prepare the soil for planting. Share the work of planting, watering, weeding, and harvesting the garden. Share a meal that includes vegetables grown in your family garden. Say: Thank You, God, for our delicious food. Thank You for our family that shared all the hard work.

Let your preschooler share extra produce with neighbors or friends. If your garden is really abundant, donate fresh produce to your church's food program, a homeless shelter, or a program that feeds the hungry.

Make Your Own Wrapping Paper

Materials: newspaper; paper grocery sacks, opened and flattened; combs; acrylic paint poured onto a paper plate; aprons; international music; permanent marker

Play the international music. Ask your preschooler to help you cover the work area with newspaper. Print a Bible thought from this book in the center of each paper sack. Let your child paint by drawing a comb through the paint, and then making designs on a sack. Work with her to paint the sacks. Let them dry and use them for wrapping paper. Point to a Bible thought, and say: When we wrap presents with this wrapping paper, we will be sharing about the Bible. The Bible tells us to share with others.

Bible Thought Candy Canes

Materials: wrapped candy canes, tape, Bible thoughts printed on strips of paper

Use a computer or typewriter to print Bible thoughts from this book. Print out the strips, and cut between each thought. Guide your child to help you tape Bible thoughts to wrapped candy canes. Display the Bible thought candy canes in a bucket or bowl. Offer the candy canes to families that visit your home. Ask your preschooler to choose one to share with you (read the Bible thought together). Let your child share the candy canes with other preschoolers at day care, preschool, or church.

Tip: See page 151 for reproducible Bible thoughts.

Hanging Out at the Mall

Turn your trip to the mall into a chance to meet and serve others. Take a break and hang out in a child play area. Let your preschooler play with other preschoolers as you visit with parents or guardians. Introduce your family members. Encourage each other as you discuss the joys and difficulties of being a parent. Suggest meeting again in the future so the children can play. Invite your new friends to attend parent-friendly services, classes, or support groups offered by your church. Share the love and acceptance of Jesus with other parents.

As you leave, say: Did you have fun? Today we shared friendship and fun with other families!

Tip: Always carry a card or flyer with church information to give to families that you meet.

Share the Music

Play your favorite music and invite your preschooler to move to the music. Hold hands and wiggle around the room. Offer scarves to your child, and let her move one to the music. Share a scarf by each of you holding one end and moving it to the music. If your preschooler is younger, hold him and sway and rock to the music. Share the joy of movement and sound as the music plays. Toddlers will enjoy bouncing up and down as they hear the beat of the music. Preschoolers of all ages like to watch their parents have fun. Involve them in the music, and have lots of fun!

Food from the Pantry

Ask your preschooler to go shopping in your pantry at home. Give her a bag and let her choose some of the packaged foods to place in the bag. Tell her that you are going to share this food with families that don't have enough food. After your child has filled the bag, go together to share the food with a local agency that helps families in need. Say: God has given us plenty of food. We are sharing our food with other families. God wants us to share what we have.

Playing at the Park

A community park or elementary school with play equipment is a perfect place to practice sharing. Take a ball, and go to the park when it is busy (not during school hours). Guide your child to share the toys and equipment. Take turns on the swing, share the slide, climb the stairs and ladders, and share the ball with other children. Discuss proper manners and how sharing and taking turns makes others feel good. Ask your child: Who wants us to share? How does God feel when we share and love others?

Share Your Feelings

Preschoolers don't always understand the way they feel. As you go about your daily schedule with your family, talk aloud about your feelings. Express when you are feeling nervous, sad, scared, frustrated, angry, happy, or excited. Let your preschooler see you experience feelings about things that happen in your life. By talking about and naming your feelings, you will help your child learn how to name and deal with his feelings. Comment on how your child is feeling, and ask if that is correct. Encourage him to tell how he feels. Say: It looks like you are feeling frustrated. Is that how you feel? May I help you with something?

Look at a family photograph. Discuss how each person in the picture might have been feeling when the picture was taken. Draw attention to pictures of babies, toddlers, and preschoolers in magazines. Look at the facial expressions of each, and talk about the way each is feeling.

Reassure your child that God gave us feelings, and He expects us to feel them! One way to help others is to share our feelings with them. After others know how we feel, we may be able to help them with a problem, offer sympathy, share their feelings, and tell them about Jesus.

Turn Off the TV

Choose one night a week to turn off the TV, VCR, video games, and anything electronic. Enjoy family time. Bring out the watercolor paints, crayons, markers, scissors, glue, and paper and have a creative fest! Or blow the dust off of the preschool board games and puzzles and play with them. Another great way to spend family time is to clean out the toy box! Sorting and organizing toys (and playing with them along the way) is a fun way to interact with your child. Who knows what exciting toys are hiding at the bottom of the toy box?

Tip: Turn your toy box cleanout into a donation time. Suggest that your child choose a few items to share with a child who is less fortunate. Donate the toys to a shelter or needy family.

Emergency Response

Read the newspaper or watch the news to find out about community emergencies that cause families to lose their homes and belongings, or medical illnesses that require community help to solve related problems. Talk with your preschooler about the situation, using only language and details that are appropriate for your child. Pray for the family members in the middle of the situation. Ask your child to help you think of a way to share what you have to provide for the needs of the people in the situation. For example, if a family loses their home in a fire, talk about things the family needs, and determine a way to share with them. Say: Jesus wants us to watch out for each other. We can show Jesus' love by sharing with other families.

Party Poppers

Materials: cardboard tubes (paper towels or toilet paper); individually wrapped candy or treats; scissors; wrapping paper; tape; labels printed with the Bible thought; curling ribbon

Make these party poppers for special occasions such as a birthday or holiday party. Choose candy and wrapping paper appropriate to the theme and age of your child.

Guide your preschooler to stuff candy into the tubes. Wrap each tube with paper. Tie ends closed with a piece of curling ribbon. Let your child tape a Bible thought on top of each tube. Arrange the poppers in a container for your special event. Ask your child to share a popper with each guest, and tell about the Bible thought.

Bible Thought: God is good to us (see Psalm 73:1).

Build a Tent

Use sheets or blankets and drape them over a table to form a tent. Put pillows, books, and a flashlight beneath the table. Crawl into the tent with your child. Play with the flashlight, and read books. Share the fun of doing something different and a little crazy! Say: This is so much fun! God wants us to share our fun with each other!

3
Caring

Read More About It: 2 Corinthians 1:3–4; Galatians 6:2,10; Ephesians 4:32; 5:1–2

Bible Thoughts for Preschoolers

Be kind to each other (see Eph. 4:32).

God cares for you (see 1 Peter 5:7).

What is caring?

Caring is showing concern or interest in another person. To care is to have an attachment to a person. Caring is showing others that we care for them personally: physically, emotionally, spiritually, and intellectually. As believers in Jesus, we are all called to care for and to express concern, interest, and love to each other.

The Bible tells us to care for each other (1 Cor. 12:25). Members of a family or church should be concerned about and extend care to each other. Caring for each other means crying together, rejoicing in happy times, sharing feelings, discussing problems, helping when needed, and being involved in the lives of others. Caring is an extension of love. When we care for others, we are tangibly showing that we love them.

As a parent, you spend much of your time caring for your preschooler and other family members. The caring you give to

38

your family is seen in hundreds of little things, like clean laundry, cooked meals, bandages on boo-boos, wiped noses, changed diapers, playtime with toys, and tucked in babies. As you care for your family, you are demonstrating love. Showing love and caring is what God wants you to do.

Why is caring important?

God has called all believers to be a light to others. He wants believers to be filled with His light, and share that light with the families around them. Caring is a very important way of sharing His light. Caring is allowing God to use our hands, feet, hearts, and resources to touch the world with His love. When we care for others, we are representing God. Others will learn about God by the things we do. Caring for others is important to God's plan for the world.

Many stories in the Bible tell of how Jesus took care of His disciples. He cared for them when they were hungry, afraid, nervous, questioning, tired, and hurting. Jesus also took care of others beyond His circle of close friends. He cared for the people He encountered. He provided food, healing, teaching, even resurrection from death. The importance of caring was evident in the life of Jesus.

We are called to care for our families and those around us. As we spend time in daily prayer and Bible reading, the Holy Spirit will reveal ways we can care for others. Pray for a caring heart and a caring spirit. Ask the Lord to show you how to care for and love your family. Let Him show you ways and open doors for caring for others outside of your family.

How can I teach my preschooler to care?

Preschoolers are very concrete in everything they do! That means they have to see examples of what they need to learn. They need to have hands-on practice of actually helping to care for someone else. The more they have their hands involved in the task of caring for someone, the better they will understand and be able to learn how to care! Think *doing, doing, doing!* (That does sound like a preschooler, doesn't it?)

When I taught preschool, three very important ideas were always in the middle of classroom activities: doing, repeating, and simple explanations. Planned activities allowed for constant doing, repeating, and explaining! Know that your child will need to experience caring activities and actions many times before he will understand. But the great thing is, as a parent, you live with your preschooler! You can teach your child about caring any time of the day or night. Your child loves and adores you, and will be tuned in to notice what you think is important—caring for others!

Invite your preschooler to help you as you care for family members. Let her help fold clothes or make beds. Assign her the task of caring for the family pet. Do household chores together, explaining that chores are one way to care for each other. Let your preschooler help as you care for others outside of your family. Take her with you when you give a meal to someone who has had surgery, or as you deliver needed items to a women's shelter. Let your child see that caring is a part of God's plan. Tell her that God wants us to care for others, and when we care for others, we are showing God's love to them.

Activities

Make the Beds

Teach your child to make his own bed. Help smooth the sheets, straighten the covers, and fluff the pillows. Slow down and enjoy the task, and show that doing chores are a nice way to care for others. Let him help you make your bed and other beds in your home. Say: We are caring for our family. When we care for others, we are showing that we love them.

Spring Pick-Me-Up

Materials: two clay pots, soil, rye grass seed, water, ribbon

Ask your child to fill the clay pots three-fourths full with soil. Cover the top of the dirt with seeds, and add another layer of soil. Give her the responsibility of watering the seeds every day. Place in a sunny, warm spot to grow. Ask: What do you think is going to happen to the seeds? After they grow, we will show we care by giving someone a pot of pretty grass.

After the rye grass is about two inches tall, help your child tie a bright length of ribbon around the pots. Place one pot on your table as a cheery decoration. Ask your preschooler to think of someone who needs cheering up, and deliver the other pot to that person. Let your child give the pot to the person. Show that you care by visiting and spending time with the person.

Feeding Fido

Give your preschooler the responsibility of caring for the family pet. Show how to feed, water, brush, walk, and care for the animal. Help your child as she learns how to perform the caring chores. Say: You are caring for Fido. When you care for something, you show that you love it!

Remind your child to care for the pet. If your child needs lots of reminders, create a chart that lists the days of the week along the top, and a simple drawing of each animal care chore along the side. Let her put a sticker or draw a happy face in the boxes as each chore is completed.

Mr. and Miss Manners

With your preschooler, open the Bible and read the Bible thoughts for this chapter. Tell your child that God cares for him. Say: The Bible tells us to be kind to each other. When we use good manners, we show kindness to others.

Make it a family goal to practice manners. Be specific as you tell your child about manners, such as saying please and thank you. Explain why each manner is important. Practice throughout the day, in different situations. Let your child repeat the words, and use them with people other than you. Compliment your child as he uses good manners.

Shop for Others

Before you go grocery shopping, think of a person who has trouble shopping. Call and offer to shop for that person (grandparent, shut-in, someone who has recently had surgery, or person without a vehicle). Let your preschooler help you make the list given by the person you are helping. Let her hold a notepad and draw pictures (or scribbles) of each item as you jot it down on a piece of paper.

When you arrive at the grocery store, give your child the job of holding the list and checking off items as you shop. Explain why you are shopping for someone else. Say: We are shopping for Mrs. Smith. She has her leg in a cast and can't get to the store. We are showing that we care for Mrs. Smith.

Let your preschooler greet your friend and help carry groceries into the house. Help put things away. Tell your friend thank you for letting you care for her. Offer to pray for your friend before you leave.

Pudding in a Cloud

Materials: favorite flavor of instant pudding, milk, mixing bowl, wire whip, spoon, whipped topping, dessert bowls

Make a special dessert with your child to show caring to your family. Use a spoon to make a nest of white whipped topping in each bowl (one for each family member). Follow package directions to make pudding. Let your child pour the pudding mix and milk into the bowl, and use the whip to stir the pudding. Carefully divide pudding between all bowls. Place in the refrigerator to chill.

After dinner, let your child surprise family members by delivering pudding in a cloud to each person. Together, say: We care for you! We love you!

Cooking with a Preschooler

Preschoolers love to cook! Cooking is a huge part of caring for others. Let your child do as much of the preparation and cooking as possible. Support your child as needed, using your hands to steady small fingers. Expect that mistakes and messes will be made, and remember messes can be cleaned up! Just as preschoolers learn by doing, they also learn from mistakes!

Some things a preschooler can do: point to the recipe, pour liquids, measure ingredients, stir, scoop, roll, pat, wash fruit and vegetables, chop soft items with a butter knife, taste, get containers or ingredients, serve food, and help wash dishes.

Do not let preschoolers work around hot surfaces, electrical appliances, or use sharp utensils.

Walking in the Rain

Gather family umbrellas and go for a walk in the rain! Put on waterproof boots and a warm jacket if necessary. Carry your younger preschooler, protecting both of you with an umbrella. Show your older child how to carefully carry the open umbrella. Look for people walking by, and wave and say hello. If a neighbor is making a mad dash for the door, offer to share an umbrella! Show caring by helping them get themselves and their belongings into their home.

Enjoy the walk in the rain. Say: God cares for all of us. He wants us to care for and be kind to each other.

Say aloud a sentence prayer that each person you meet will want to hear about Jesus.

Greeting Cards for Shut-ins

Materials: empty thread spools, acrylic paint poured on paper plates, apron, cardstock cut in half and folded into cards, invitation envelopes, pen, bag

Make greeting cards. Show your child how to dip a spool into paint and stamp a design on front of the cards. Encourage him to cover the entire front with spool prints. Dry. On the inside of each card, print a Bible thought from this book. On the back cover, let your child print his first name. Collect cards and an equal number of envelopes together and place in a bag. With your preschooler, visit a homebound person from your church or neighborhood. Let your child give the cards to the person. Share how Jesus has recently blessed your life. Ask your child to share how he made the cards.

Pack a Lunch

Show care for your spouse. Invite your preschooler to help you pack a lunch for the next day. Prepare lunch favorites, such as a sub sandwich, veggies and dip, a boiled egg, a cold drink, and a special dessert. Give your child the lunch sack or a piece of paper and let her use markers to decorate the bag or draw a love picture. Print your own love message on the bag or the picture. Place all items in the bag, and fold the top closed. Punch two holes in the top, thread a piece of ribbon through the holes, and tie a bow. Place in the refrigerator. Tell your spouse to look in the refrigerator. Say: We care for you! We made you a surprise lunch for tomorrow!

Shoebox of Cookies for Firefighters

Bake a batch of your favorite cookies with your preschooler. Line a shoebox with aluminum foil, and fill with cookies. Cover the cookies with foil, replace the lid, and tape shut. Wrap the box with plain paper and tape. Give your child markers and stickers and let him decorate the box. Deliver the shoebox to your local fire station. Talk with the fire chief, and tell how much you appreciate the hard work of the firefighters. Let your child tell the firefighters thank you. Offer to pray for the firefighters, their safety, and their families.

As you leave, tell your child that firefighters care for others. Say: Firefighters help other people. They want to keep families safe.

Hint: Call ahead and ask if someone is available to give you and your child a tour of the fire station.

Bible Thought Houseplant Flags

Materials: wooden skewers, triangular pieces of paper, permanent pen, markers, tape, bushy houseplant

Use the permanent pen to print a Bible thought from this book on each piece of paper. Ask your preschooler to color on the flags while you read the Bible thoughts. Let your child help you tape each flag on the dull end of a skewer. Stick the Bible thought flags into the dirt of the plant and place the plant on the table. During meals, ask your child to name a color, and read that Bible thought. Tell your child that the Bible tells us to care for each other.

Blocks Are Fun

Time to dig out the wooden blocks! Make a pile of all of the blocks your child has. Sit in the middle of the floor, and spend quality time playing with your child. Build towers, bridges, houses, long rows, and shapes. Or make patterns and designs with the colored blocks. Show your child that you care by joining in his play. Say: I love you! I care for you. What do you want to build next?

Tip: Choose your child's favorite toy for playtime. Babies will enjoy plastic snap beads or a teething ring. Toddlers will have fun putting blocks into a wide-mouthed plastic container. Older preschoolers enjoy challenging puzzles or simple board games.

Pick Up the Trash

Make your neighborhood a prettier place to be. Help your child put on rubber or work gloves. Carry a garbage bag as you walk around your neighborhood. Work together with your preschooler to gather trash. Watch for sharp or dangerous items, and advise your child to let you pick up those things. Have a game to see who can find the most trash. Celebrate when your bag is full. Toss the garbage in a dumpster or garbage can. As you wash hands afterwards, say: We showed caring for others by making the neighborhood look nice and clean.

What's Your Favorite Music?

Music is a wonderful way to show caring. Keep a selection of preschool and Christian music in the car. As you drive to the store, school, day care, or work, invite your child to choose what type of music to listen to. Allowing your child to make choices is an important way to show caring. Preschoolers love to experience the independence of making a choice. Take turns choosing music. Enjoy listening and singing along with the songs. Say: I'm glad you chose that music! I love the words, and the bouncy music!

Family Pajama Movie Night

Choose one night of the week to be family pajama movie night. Let each family member take a turn to be the person in charge of choices for the evening. Let your preschooler be the first to be in charge of choices. After everyone puts on pajamas, let him choose a movie, the snack, the drinks, and the seating arrangement. Teach caring by letting him have a turn, and then letting him follow the choices that others make. Say: We show others that we care when we let them make choices. In our family, we take turns making choices.

Flowers for the Pastor

Let your child help you cut a bunch of flowers from your garden, select a bunch from the grocery store, or draw a bouquet of flowers with markers and crayons. Place fresh flowers in a container filled with cool water. Mount a drawing of flowers on a piece of construction paper. Print a message to your pastor on a notecard or the back of the drawing. Tell your child that giving gifts is one way to show caring for others. Say: Our pastor cares for us. We will show him that we care when we give him these flowers. We will tell him thank you for taking care of us.

Deliver the flowers and card with your preschooler.

Family Love Letters

Materials: colorful paper, scissors, glue sticks, stickers, markers, colored pencils, paper scraps

Have a family love letter afternoon. Lay materials on a table, and encourage each person to create a love letter to the family. Chop pieces of paper scraps and glue them to a piece of brightly colored paper. Draw pictures, scribble messages, and print words said by your preschooler. When the love letters are complete, cuddle up on the couch and share the love letters with each other. Let family members show they care by giving a love letter and telling how they feel about each other. Say: We care for each other. God cares for us!

Play in the Sandbox

Go to a city park, beach, or play area that has a sand area. Take a plastic tub filled with plastic buckets, containers, cups, and spoons. Play in the sand with your child. Encourage her to share sand toys with other boys and girls. Show caring by how you interact with your child and the other children. Help the boys and girls share the toys and play together. Say: It's nice when we play together. God wants us to be kind to each other.

Chocolate-Filled Cloud

Materials: large plastic egg, silver foil covered chocolate kisses or candy, glue, cotton balls, wet washcloth, waxed paper, piece of paper with the Bible thought written on it

Place the open egg halves face down on the wax paper. Show your preschooler how to use his finger to smear glue on the outside of the egg. Wipe sticky fingers on the damp towel. Stick cotton balls all over the glue-covered egg. Dry. Turn the egg halves over, and let your child fill one half with chocolate kisses. Place the Bible thought inside, and close the egg. Ask your child: Who can we give this egg to? Let's think of someone who needs to be encouraged or cheered up.

Let your preschooler give the egg to the chosen person. Say: We care for you.

Bible Thought: God cares for you (see 1 Peter 5:7).

Swinging at the Park

Play with your child on your swing set, or take a trip to a playground that has swings. Show your child you care by focusing all of your attention and energy on him. Push him on the swings. Go down the slide. Climb the playground equipment. Challenge him to do new things. Cheer him on when he succeeds. Say: I care for you! I love you! I'm glad God game me such a wonderful child.

Caring for Others

Each community has families that need extra caring. Look in the phone book, or ask neighbors or church leaders for ideas. Perhaps your church serves meals for the homeless, has a food pantry, an afterschool program, or a clothes closet to care for others.

As a family, choose a charity or service group to support. Call the office of your chosen group, and ask for a list of needs. Discuss the needs and the list with your family. Include your preschooler (even babies like to be a part of family discussions)

in the discussion. Decide how you can help your charity group. Perhaps you can volunteer by serving meals, purchasing toiletries, collecting resources, or donating used clothing or bedding items. Work together as a family to gather items or serve others. Deliver the items to the program. Let each family member be a part of giving the items or helping the program. Say: We are showing that we care by giving to other people. They will know we care because we are helping them.

Yard Work

Work together as a family in caring for your yard (or your house, apartment, car, or other possession that needs care). Spend time outside, pulling weeds, planting flowers, picking up garbage, mowing the grass, or doing what needs to be done. Babies can participate by playing in a playpen or sitting on a blanket to watch you work. Toddlers and older preschoolers can pull a supply wagon, deliver flowers to plant, or water flowers. Give each family member a job. When the yard work is complete, sit on a blanket and enjoy the beautiful yard. Share a snack and drink. Pray aloud, and thank God for a caring family.

Diaper Time

Diaper time comes several times a day (and night). Show caring for you baby or toddler during diaper time. Make a special diaper changing area in your home. Include diaper-changing supplies, colorful pictures, a bright mobile, and source of music. Enjoy the time spent changing diapers! Make eye contact, sing along with the music, make the mobile move, and love your baby! Your child will learn how to care by being cared for.

4

Praying

Read More About It: Acts 6:4; Ephesians 6:18; Philippians 4:6–7; 1 Timothy 2:1

Bible Thoughts for Preschoolers

Jesus prayed (see Matt. 14:23).

Pray for one another (see James 5:16).

What is prayer?

Prayer is conversation with God, talking with and listening to Him. Prayer is a time of sharing with God our concerns and worries, our joys and thanksgiving, our love and worship. We can talk with God anywhere, anytime. God wants to have conversation with us. All we have to do is start talking!

The Bible tells us to "pray without ceasing" (1 Thess. 5:17). That means talking with God all day and night, just like He is right there beside us! When we have a conversation with our friends and family, there are times of speaking and of listening. It's the same with God. Sometimes we do the talking, sometimes the listening. The more we pray, the easier it gets to talk with God and hear His voice.

There are different kinds of prayers. There is quiet prayer that builds a relationship with God. There are prayers at mealtime, bedtime, church, and emergencies. There are sentence prayers, when we utter simple phrases for what is on our heart. But each kind of prayer is just that—prayer. God wants to hear from us all the time, about every little and every big thing in our lives.

Why is prayer important?

Do you recognize your child's voice? Can you hear a baby crying, and know it's your baby? I've watched as a child utters a simple "Mommy" or "Daddy." All motion ceases, and heads turn and tune in to the child. Prayer is one way we learn to recognize God's voice. We learn to tune in to His voice in a world of loud distractions. We utter a simple "Father," "God," or "Jesus," and have His instant love and attention.

The Bible tells all believers to pray. Throughout the Bible, people spent time talking to God. Several instances are recorded of times when Jesus prayed. That's how important prayer is. Even God's Son, Jesus, needed to spend time with God in prayer. Jesus showed us how to pray, and we must follow His example.

Jesus needed prayer to build His relationship with God. From His prayers, Jesus gained love, wisdom, strength, encouragement, help, comfort, and guidance. Jesus relied on prayer to keep Him going through the struggles of daily life. He wants us to rely on prayer to get through the trials of daily life with our energetic preschoolers! Each day, we have to feed our preschoolers to keep their bodies going and growing. We also need to give them spiritual food, to keep them going and growing spiritually. Prayer is an important way to get spiritual food from God.

How can I teach my preschooler to pray?

Our job as Christian parents is to teach our preschoolers how to pray. We must model simple prayers, and give opportunities for participation in prayer. Preschoolers need to hear us pray at different times of the day, during a variety of situations. They need real examples of talking to God, who loves us and wants to talk to us—even if our words are not perfect or our eyes are not closed!

One way to teach how to pray is to pray for your child. Pray simply. Ask God for help with a situation or need; say thank you; and end with "In Jesus' name, Amen." Or offer a sentence prayer, and let the child repeat the words after you. For example: "Jesus, please help Emily's tummy feel better. Thank you. Amen." Preschoolers will learn that God wants to hear what we say, however we say it.

Preschoolers are concrete learners; they need to experience prayer. It is easier for them to pray for things they can see, smell, touch, taste, or hear. As you go about your day, comment on what God has done. "Thank You, God, for these tasty oranges," or "I'm so glad that God gave me hands to play with trucks!" Once preschoolers get the hang of praying, they will pray for and about ANYTHING! That's OK, even if the prayers seem silly to us, they are not silly to God. He enjoys our preschoolers as much as we do!

The best way to teach your family to pray is to spend time praying! Preschoolers and children of all ages are great imitators. Pray for other people, the sick, the poor, the lost, family, and friends. Babies will not understand as much as a kindergarten-age child, but both will learn the importance of prayer and talking with God from your example.

Encourage your preschooler to participate in family prayertime. Accept whatever prayer your child offers and give sincere praise when a child makes an effort to pray out loud. God easily understands the mumbled or confused prayers of our young ones! He reads the intent of our heart, not the perfection of our words.

So, start praying! Begin a lifestyle of prayer today, for you and your family.

Activities

Pray for Your Family

Display a family photograph or photos of family members on the kitchen table. At breakfast, lead a short prayer for family members and the new day ahead. Say: Jesus, please be with our family today. Keep us safe. Show us how to help someone today. Amen.

As you go about your busy day, say a short sentence prayer about a family member whenever you see the photos: Thank You, God, for Sammy's beautiful smile; or Jesus, please help Michael have a good day at school. At the end of the day, ask who was able to help someone else.

Tip: A fun activity is to let your preschooler draw the family picture! Use crayons or markers. Date the picture. Try to do a new family drawing at least once a year. It is fun to see how preschoolers grow over time and learn new skills!

Refrigerator Photo of Pastor and Family

Materials: digital or film camera, construction paper, markers, double-sided tape, magnets

Call the pastor of your church and ask permission to take a family photo following a church service. Let your preschooler talk on the phone and tell that the photo will be used for a prayer magnet. Take the photograph and have it developed.

Help your preschooler use double-sided tape to secure the photo to a piece of construction paper. Work together with markers to decorate around the photo. Let your child attach the prayer photo to the refrigerator with a magnet.

Say: This picture will remind us to pray for our pastor and his family. When we see the picture, we can say a prayer for the people in the picture. Thank You, Jesus, for our pastor and his family. Keep them healthy and safe. In Jesus' name, Amen.

Hint: Preschoolers love being in pictures. Take pictures of the pastor, his family, and your family members. Make extra prints to share with the pastor.

Sky Praying

Ask your preschooler to help you spread a quilt or sleeping bag on your lawn or somewhere in your yard. Lie on your backs on the quilt. Look at the sky (day or night) and enjoy the time resting together. Let your child point to and name things she sees. Talk about how God made the sky, the sun, the clouds, the stars, the moon, the grass, or anything else your child points to. Say: Thank You, God, for making these wonderful things!

Handprint Bulletin Board

Materials: cork bulletin board, white and blue acrylic paint, paintbrushes, aprons, newspaper, index cards, markers, pushpins, nail, hammer

Spread newspaper on a table. Put on aprons and let your preschooler paint the bulletin board blue. If your child is too young to paint alone, help hold the paintbrush and paint the board. When the board is dry, paint your child's hand white. Make white handprints all over the blue board (reapply paint to hand as needed). Wash child's hand immediately.

Let the bulletin board dry. Ask your child to hold the board as you select a spot to hang it. Work together to attach the board to the wall with the nail and hammer.

Use markers to draw pictures of people who need prayer on the index cards. Ask older children to print a prayer request or the name of the person on each card. Let your preschooler attach prayer cards to the bulletin board with pushpins. Say a prayer for the person listed on each card. Add new prayer requests as necessary. Remove answered prayer requests and say: Thank You, God, for answering these prayers!

Tip: Place the board at preschooler's eye level, making sure that toddlers and babies cannot reach it to pull off pushpins. Placing the bulletin board at preschooler's eye level will keep preschoolers interested in the display.

Pray with Your Eyes Open

Tell your preschooler that praying is talking to God, and we can talk with God anytime, anywhere. Share that God likes to hear us talk to Him, even when our eyes are open! Say: God loves it when we talk to Him. He wants to hear about everything! He even likes it when we talk to Him with our eyes open!

Let your preschooler hear you make comments to God throughout the day, as you go about your daily schedule. Let him see that talking to God is a natural act, as simple as talking aloud.

Ticktacktoe Prayer Game

Materials: masking tape, vegetable cans or wooden blocks, beanbag

Make a child-size ticktacktoe board on the floor with masking tape. Let your preschooler toss the beanbag onto the game board. Guide your child to stand or sit in the square with the beanbag and ask her to name a family member or friend. Repeat the name as a sentence prayer. Say: God, please help Molly as she gets well from chicken pox!

Give your preschooler a can or block to place in that square. Take turns tossing the beanbag, aiming for empty squares. Say a sentence prayer for someone as each square is hit. Make prayer fun. Enjoy the game and your family time!

Roll the Ball and Pray

Sit on the floor and roll a beach ball back and forth to your child. Say a sentence prayer each time one of you catches the ball. Thank God for times spent together as a family.

Cookies, a Card, and a Prayer

Materials: cookies, markers, construction paper, heart stickers, paper lunch sack, stapler

Use markers to decorate a cookie bag and greeting card. Show how to draw lines to create plaid designs on the bag and one side of the construction paper. Fold the paper in half to make a card. Let your child decorate the plaid designs with heart stickers. Print a message inside the card to a person who is ill, in the hospital, or homebound. Let your child fill the sack with cookies. Fold the sack closed, and staple the card to the top.

As a family, deliver the cookie bag to the recipient. Let your preschooler participate by giving the bag to the recipient and sharing in the conversation. Keep the visit short, and offer to pray for the person you are visiting. As you leave, compliment your child for helping someone feel better by offering prayer, a visit, and a treat.

Tip: Call ahead to arrange a good time for your visit. If you are unable to schedule a visit, leave the cookie bag and card at the door, nurses station, or give to a relative to deliver.

Caution: If you are visiting someone at the hospital, make sure it is appropriate for a child to accompany you. If your preschooler cannot go with you, tell about the visit when you return home.

Look in the Mirror and Pray

Preschoolers love looking at themselves in the mirror. Stand or sit in front of a large mirror. Point to family members in the mirror, naming each. Say a sentence prayer thanking God for making each person special. Encourage your preschooler to repeat your sentence prayer, or say his own. Smile and make silly faces in the mirror. Enjoy this time of family prayer.

Family Prayer Cards Game

Give each family member a large index card. Spend time decorating the cards with markers, crayons, stickers, rubber stamps, or whatever art supplies you have. Let each person print his name on the card.

Establish a weekly prayertime for your family. Use the decorated cards as guides. Lay the cards facedown, and let each person choose a card. Take turns saying short sentence prayers for each person. Model prayers for preschoolers, and let them repeat what you say. Soon, they will be thinking up their own sentence prayers! Say: Thank You, God, that Sebastian has a new tooth! or Please, God, help Samantha get over her cold!

Pray at Mealtime

Begin a family tradition of praying at mealtime. Say a simple prayer that thanks God for the delicious food you are going to eat. Use this regular prayertime to practice folding hands together and closing eyes for prayer. Let a different family member pray for each meal. Or designate a certain chair as "the prayer chair" and ask whoever sits in that chair to say a prayer for the meal. Be bold and pray when your family eats at restaurants or places other than your home. Show others that your family is thankful to God for the food you eat.

Pray Around the World

Materials: world map that shows each country in a different color, red paper, child-safe scissors, picture gum (poster putty)

Display the world map on a wall. Give your preschooler red paper, and help him cut small pieces.

Each day, ask your child to point to a place on the map. Read the country name. Let your preschooler roll a small piece of picture gum into a ball, attach it to the back of a piece of red paper, and stick it on the country. Pray that the people in that country will hear about and love Jesus. Tell that God made the world and all the people that live on it.

Note: This is recommended only for kindergarten-age preschoolers.

Clean Water

Ask your preschooler to help pour cold water into clear glasses. Serve the clear, clean water with dinner. Talk about the taste of the water, and what it would be like if you didn't have clean water to drink. Let your child repeat this prayer as you say: Dear Jesus, Please help missionaries have clean drinking water. Thank You. Amen.

Share that a missionary is someone who helps others and tells about Jesus. Talk about the many uses of water. Tell that some places in the world do not have safe, clean drinking water, and the people need prayers for good water.

Take a Prayerwalk

Go for a walk around your neighborhood. Smile and greet each person you see. Play a game to see who can greet the most people first, or who can smile and wave the most. As you enjoy the time together, say: Jesus, we pray that one day we will be able to tell these people about You, and they will love You like we do! Caution: If your preschooler is old enough to understand, explain the difference between greeting strangers when accompanied by a parent and talking to strangers when alone.

Prayer Tree

Materials: sturdy tree branch with many small branches, large coffee can, wrapping paper, tape, gravel, clothespins, paper heart shapes, markers, pictures of family members

Help your child tape wrapping paper around the coffee can. Hold the branch upright in the can while your child fills the can with gravel. Use clothespins to clip family photos on the tree. Print on the heart shapes the names of other people who need prayer. Let preschoolers clip the heart shapes to the tree. Put the prayer tree on a table. During family prayertime, let each child remove one heart and pray for that person. Help younger preschoolers read the name and say a prayer. Add more heart shapes as needed.

Holiday Tip: Attach Christmas cards received by your family to the prayer tree. Remove one each day and pray for the sender of the card.

Zipped Bag Missionary Prayers

Materials: resealable plastic bags, child-safe scissors, magazines, glue sticks, construction paper cut to fit inside bags, clothespin

Look through magazines and help your child cut out pictures that show the needs of missionaries and believers in Christ. Some needs are food, transportation, homes, water, health, safety, families, work, the Bible, Jesus, sleep, school, and fun. Let your child glue pictures on construction paper. Place in plastic bags and zip. Use a clothespin to clip together several bags.

Each day, choose a different bag. With your child, look at the pictures on the card and pray for missionaries and believers around the world. Say: Today you chose pictures of food. Dear Jesus, help everyone who serves You and helps others have good food to eat. Thank You. Amen.

Remember: A missionary is a believer who serves and helps others. All believers are missionaries and are to serve and help other people. Your preschooler may not understand or be able to say the word *missionary*, but he will be hearing and learning about being more like Jesus.

Prayer Bible Thoughts

Use your family Bible to look up the Bible thoughts in this chapter about prayer. Read the Bible thoughts to your preschooler. For older preschoolers, print the Bible thoughts on index cards and let your child attach them to a dresser drawer or bedroom door. Help your child point to and read the words. Talk about Jesus and praying for others. Say: Thank You, God, for the Bible that teaches us about prayer.

ABC Prayers

Display an ABC poster in your home. Place a spiral notebook and markers near the poster. On the first day, ask your preschooler to think of a word that begins with A, such as *airplane, apple,* or *ant.* Let her (help if necessary) copy the letter on the first page of the notebook. Print the word she has chosen and help draw a picture of the word. Lead your child to pray for the chosen word and others. Say: Dear Jesus, please help families that fly on airplanes be safe. Amen.

Pray through the alphabet, one letter a day. Skip a notebook page between each letter. When you finish the alphabet, you can start again by adding a different word for each letter. Your child will be proud of the prayer alphabet book she has helped make. Hint: For younger preschoolers, point to an alphabet picture and say a sentence prayer about the picture.

Summertime Prayer Fans

Materials: cardstock, child-safe scissors, crayons, paint-stirring sticks, permanent marker, glue gun

Make a pattern for a prayer fan. Trace several and help your child cut them out. Decorate one side of each fan with crayons. On the blank side, print: *Pray that missionaries and families who have preschoolers will love Jesus.* Hot glue the decorated fans to sticks. Give the fans to extended family members or place on church pews for use during church services.

Caution: Keep glue gun out of reach of preschoolers.

Pray at Play

Show your child that play and prayer can happen at the same time. Play with your child. Say a sentence prayer for your child as she plays. Say: Father, thank You that Suzy loves to share her toys. Amen.

Say a sentence prayer aloud each time you see your child playing.

Prayer Notes

Fold pieces of construction paper in half. Let family members decorate the outside with rubber stamps, a stamp pad, and colored pencils.

Ask your preschooler to name someone he would like to pray for and why. Print a message inside a decorated prayer note, saying that your family has prayed for that person. Let family members print their names on the card. Work together to put the card in an envelope, address it, add a stamp, and put it in the mailbox. Say a prayer as you mail the card.

Bedtime Prayers

Prayer at bedtime is a perfect way to wrap up the day, a special time between you, your preschooler, and God. Sit with your child, and pray together about the day. Keep the prayertime simple and conversation-like. Let your preschooler thank God for what she thinks was special about the day, and ask prayers for those in her thoughts. Bedtime prayers are calming and will give you a chance to connect with your child after a busy day.

5

Giving

Read More About It: 2 Corinthians 8:3–4; 2 Corinthians 9:6–8; 1 John 3:17–19

Bible Thoughts for Preschoolers

Give thanks to the Lord for He is good (see Psalm 107:1).

God loves a cheerful giver (see 2 Cor. 9:7).

What is giving?

Giving is an act of presenting something to another person. To give means to present something without expecting anything in return: not a gift, money, a hug, or even a thank-you. The list of things to give is endless: time, energy, money, presents, love, friendship, food, clothes, help, forgiveness . . . In church settings, many people think giving is only important when money is given. Giving money is one way to support God's plan to share Jesus with the people of the world. But we should also give our time, our talents, and our resources.

The Bible tells us to be cheerful givers (2 Cor. 9:7). When my teenagers were preschoolers, I loved giving gifts or helping with a project. I was able to give them something tangible, like a toy, or my assistance building a playhouse from a cardboard box. I enjoyed surprising them, and they delighted in being the recipients of giving. I wasn't always cheerful, since many days as a parents of a preschooler are anything but calm and stress-free! But I loved my children, and they knew that I was happy to give to them. I never begrudged the time, money, or energy I gave to my preschoolers. That's what is meant by being a cheerful giver. Give joyfully, expecting nothing in return.

Why is giving important?

The Bible instructs us to give and take care of each other. When we follow what the Bible says, we are being obedient to God. When we are obedient, we will grow spiritually and be blessed by God. God will take care of our needs.

What is important about giving is the act itself. Giving demonstrates unselfishness. When we give away our time, our money, our resources, or ourselves, we are showing trust in God. We show that we trust God to give us what we need in our daily lives. Giving is an expression of our thankfulness to God for what He has given us. It is an acknowledgment that He provides everything we have.

As parents, we give a home, food, clothes, toys, education, health care, even vacations and playtime to our children. Any exhausted parent can testify that we give to our families! Our preschoolers will grow up knowing and trusting that they will be cared for. When they see us give unselfishly, they will be witnesses to a wonderful example of giving. They will see giving in action.

How can I teach my preschooler to give?

For a child to learn to give, she must see examples of giving and have opportunities to practice giving. We've heard "practice makes perfect." We know we can never be perfect, since Jesus is the only perfect One! But if we want to become really good at giving, we have to practice, practice, practice!

Nurture a giving attitude in your child. Younger preschoolers have to practice giving by sharing toys and belongings. Help your child see the needs of others. Point out another child who doesn't have a toy, and suggest your child give one to that child. Look for people who lack clothing or food, and let your child watch you find a way to give needed items. Notice a person who needs your energy and time, and willingly give both in the presence of your child. Practice tithing at church, and let your child place the envelope in the offering plate. Pay attention to special offerings collected to help others who tell about Jesus. As you give money to help, tell your child about the importance of why you are giving. Gather food, clothing, or household items to donate to your church or a local help agency. Show cheerfulness and willingness to give to others the things they need.

The best way to teach your child how to give is to involve him in your giving. Let him carry a bag of groceries to the food collection box. Let him put money in the special bank or look to see who doesn't have a toy. Let him help you give time picking up trash for a neighbor. Your preschooler will learn from your examples and love being involved in your lifestyle of giving of yourself, your time, your money, and your energy.

Activities

Jesus Loves You Heart Pocket

Materials: construction paper, scissors, stapler, hole punch, yarn, marker, heart stickers, candy

Place your hand over your child's and draw a large heart on construction paper. Together, hold two sheets and cut two hearts at one time. Staple the hearts together. Punch holes around the bottom two-thirds of the heart. Cut a long piece of yarn, and help your child sew around the heart, leaving extra yarn on both ends. Tie the yarn ends together to form a loop for hanging. Print the

Bible thought on one side of the heart. Ask your child to decorate the other side with stickers and markers, and fill the heart with candy. Let your preschooler give the heart to a parent or grandparent, and say: Jesus loves you. I love you!

Bible Thought: Jesus loves you (see John 15:12).

Rock-a-Bye Baby

Gently rock your baby. As you rock, give her your total attention and love. Gaze into her eyes and snuggle. Nuzzle her cheek and hold her tiny fingers. Softly sing "Jesus Loves the Little Children." Focus on your baby, putting away other cares. Give the gift of time and love!

Recycle and Save

Recycle your trash and save money for a special need or offering! With your child, gather boxes. Label boxes with a piece of paper that says what type of item to put in each: soft drink cans, plastic bottles, glass, and newspapers. Place the boxes in a garage or protected area of your yard. Say: Let's recycle our trash. When the boxes are full, we will take them to the recycling center and get money for them. We can give the money for a special offering!

Teach your child what to recycle. Show how to rinse plastic, glass, and aluminum containers and place in the proper box. Let him stack newspaper in its box. Let your child help deliver the recyclables. Give him the money to put in an envelope. Choose the recipient of the money saved from recycling, and cheerfully give to the cause.

Teacher, What Do You Need?

Ask your child's teacher or day-care provider if she has any needs for her classroom. Perhaps she needs snack items, cutting magazines, glue, a game, or a toy. With your preschooler, shop for or gather needed items. If you are purchasing something, give the money or check to your preschooler to pay for the item. Say: We are giving this to your teacher. She needs our help. She will be so happy when we give this to her!

Let your preschooler deliver the needed item.

Volunteer at Day Care or Preschool

Schedule a day to volunteer at your child's day care or preschool. Talk with your child before the scheduled day, and say: I am going to give my time to your teacher. I'm going to help at your school!

On the volunteer day, cheerfully give your time and energy to do whatever needs to be done—read books with preschoolers, play in the dress up area, build block towers, or run the painting center. Show by your smile and attitude that it is fun to give to others.

Bake Two, Take One

Plan a family cooking night. Choose a favorite pie recipe, and gather the necessary supplies and ingredients to make two pies. Pop a favorite music CD into the stereo, and work away! Together, prepare the pies. Let your preschooler help as much as possible. Let her chop, roll, fill, wash dishes, or anything else she is able to do. While the pies are baking, clean the kitchen and sing along with the music. Say: We made two pies. We will eat one and give one. Who should we give the other pie to?

Discuss possible pie recipients. After the pie has cooled, go as a family to deliver the pie. Visit and spend a short time enjoying friendship.

Nature Walk

Take a plastic bag, wear good walking shoes, and go for a nature walk with your preschooler. Walk in a nearby park, through part of a forest, or along a beach. Share how God gave us a beautiful world. Collect nature items like pine cones, rocks, sticks, shells, leaves, or nuts and put them in the bag.

After returning home, let your child choose some of the items to give to a friend. Say: I think Tommy will be happy when you give him that shell! Jesus is happy when we give to others.

Buy One, Get One Free

Your older preschooler will enjoy reading the grocery ads in the newspaper with you, and helping you locate buy one, get one free deals. Make a list of good deals and go shopping. Let your child place the bought items in your pantry, and the free items in a bag. Give the bag of free things to a needy family, a homeless shelter, or a church food pantry. Tell your child that some people do not have jobs or do not make enough money to buy the food they need. Say: Jesus wants us to take care of each other. We are giving food for people who are hungry.

Lollipop Walk

Purchase a bag of individually wrapped sugar-free lollipops. On a computer, print strips of paper that say *Jesus Loves You!* Cut the strips apart, and ask your preschooler to stamp hearts or flowers on the paper strips. Fold the strips in half, and tape one to each lollipop stick or wrapper. Let your child put the lollipops in a basket. Go for a walk around the neighborhood. Tell your preschooler to offer a lollipop to children you meet. As your child offers a lollipop, say: We have a treat for you. Jesus loves you!

Bible Thought Bible Markers

Most craft stores have wonderful selections of scrapbook paper. Allow each family member to choose a sheet of paper. Cut the paper into bookmark strips. On the back of each, print one of the Bible thoughts listed in this book. Older preschoolers and children can print their own Bible thoughts. Locate the Bible thoughts in your family Bible, read them, and mark the place with a bookmark. Keep the Bible on a coffee table so younger preschoolers can learn to gently turn the pages and find their Bible thoughts.

Tip: Use Bible thought bookmarks to mark other books that family members are reading.

Lemonade Stand

Materials: table, chairs, shade umbrella, lemonade (recipe follows) in insulated cooler, ice, scoop, cups, sign that says *Get Your Ice Cold Lemonade Here*, masking tape, coffee can covered with construction paper, marker

Before the lemonade day, choose a special project that needs money, such as an offering, a missions project, or a church need.

Choose a warm, sunny day to sell lemonade. Arrange the table, chairs, and umbrella. Hang the sign from the edge of the table. Print *Donations* on the coffee can and place it on the table near the lemonade, cups, and ice. Let your child scoop ice into a few cups and fill them with lemonade. Offer lemonade to people as they walk by. Tell about the special project you are supporting with the donations given. Visit with your child and customers.

Let your preschooler give the money to the person in charge of the chosen project. Say: God, thank You that we can give this money to help.

SPARKLING LEMONADE

Powdered presweetened lemonade mix
1 lemon per 2-quart container of lemonade
Sparkling water or ginger ale

Follow directions on lemonade mix packet, substituting half of the water with sparkling water. Cut a lemon in half and squeeze fresh juice into the container. Stir and pour into insulated container. Serve by pouring lemonade over ice.

An Apple for the Mail Carrier

Let your preschooler wash and polish an apple. Wrap it in a piece of tissue paper or colored plastic wrap and a piece of yarn or ribbon. Print a short thank-you note to your mail carrier. Ask your preschooler to place the note and apple in your mailbox. Say: It's nice to surprise people with a gift. How do you think our mail carrier will feel when she gets this surprise? Thank You, Jesus, for those who help us.

Note: If you receive your mail at the post office, let your child give the gift to the person helping customers.

Soup Mix Gift Jar

Materials: clean, quart glass jar with a lid; small plastic bag; tape; 1/2 cup each of four types of dried beans, such as pinto, black, kidney, or black-eyed peas; 1/2 cup uncooked rice; 2 tablespoons chili powder; 2 beef bullion cubes; 1 tablespoon parsley flakes; 1 tablespoon onion flakes; 1 teaspoon each black pepper, salt, garlic powder; directions printed on an index card

Let your child layer dried beans and rice in the jar. Place dried spices and unwrapped bullion cubes in the plastic bag. Place the spice packet on top of the beans, and close the jar. Tape the directions to the jar. Go with your preschooler to give the soup mix to a church or community leader. Let your child tell the leader that his hard work is appreciated.

Directions: Fill a large soup pan with 4 quarts of water. Bring to a boil, and add dried beans and rice. Cover, turn down heat, and simmer for 30 minutes, stirring often. Add water if needed. Add spice packet, stir, and continue cooking until beans are soft, at least 30 minutes.

If desired, top with sour cream or grated cheese. This soup is delicious served with corn bread. Enjoy!

Ring Around the Family

Hold hands and move around in a circle, singing the song. At the end of the song, fall down on soft ground or carpet. Give hugs, and play again. To the tune of "Ring Around the Rosy," sing:

Ring around the family,

A pocket full of love-ies,

Kisses, kisses,

We all fall down!

Say: I love you!

Car Wash

Materials: hose with spray nozzle hooked to water source; towels; bucket with soapy water; large sponges or rags for washing

Wash the family car. Let your child wash with a sponge and dry with a towel. Watch for neighbors who stop to visit. Offer to wash their cars! Show your preschooler that doing something nice for others is fun. Fellowship with the neighbors as you wash their car.

Seasonal Door Decoration

Use your front door or porch as a display of thankfulness for what God has given your family. Let your preschooler and family members help decorate the area with seasonal items. For example, for fall, display cornstalks, pumpkins, gourds, squash, and dried fall flowers. Use markers or paints to make a sign that says *Thank You, God, for giving us food to harvest*! Let your preschooler decorate the borders of the sign. Attach it to the cornstalks or to a wooden stake and stand it in the display. Say: God gives us food that we need. Thank You, God, for giving to us.

Change the display for different holidays or seasons. Always include a sign that tells guests and neighbors what the Lord has done for your family.

Food Drive

Plan a food drive for the needy in your area. Work with your church family or neighborhood families. Make copies of the Food Drive flyer on page 154. With your preschooler and other family members, cut pictures of food items from the newspaper or magazine ads. Glue one food picture on each flyer. Fill in the blanks that tell where and when the food will be collected, who it will be given to, and contact information.

Let your preschooler give the flyers to families at church, or walk with you in your neighborhood, delivering them door-to-door. On the assigned day, ask your preschooler to help gather donated food items and place them in boxes. As you work together, talk about how people give resources to help others. Say: We will give this food to families who don't have enough to eat. I'm glad we can help God give to others.

Include your preschooler as you deliver the food items to your chosen charity.

Give a Flower, Give a Smile

Materials: small glass jar, pieces of ribbon, cut flowers, water

Walk with your preschooler and pick several flowers and some greenery from your garden. Or, choose a bunch of flowers at a store. Let your child arrange a few flowers and a bit of greenery in a jar filled with water. Help tie a bow of ribbon around the jar rim. Visit a neighbor, a shut-in, or a grandparent and let your child give the flower jar and a big smile to the person you are visiting. Talk about the beautiful flowers that God made and the beautiful smile that God gave.

A Treat for You

Plan a special surprise with your child. With your preschooler, bake or purchase a favorite family dessert or candy. Hide the treat until after dinner. As a family, clear the table, and then ask your child to announce that it's time for a surprise! Ask everyone to close their eyes, and let your preschooler give each family member a dessert (or candy on a napkin). After she has given each a treat, let her say: Surprise! Open your eyes. I love you!

Water Giveaway

Attend a summer community parade, sporting event, or fair prepared to give away cold water. Let your preschooler help you fill a red wagon with ice and nestle sealed bottles of water in the ice. Pull the wagon to your vantage point. Enjoy the event. As hot families pass by, let your child ask if they would like ice-cold water. Help if necessary. If the families say thank you, say: You are welcome. Jesus loves you!

Be ready to share about Jesus if the people ask questions.

Give a Bible

Teach your preschooler the importance of having and using a Bible. Make sure each family member has an age-appropriate Bible, and remind them to carry it to church. Use each child's Bible to look up Bible thoughts. Ask church leaders if your church has a program to give Bibles to guests or needy families. As a family, donate money to purchase Bibles for this program. If your church does not have a Bible giveaway program, go to a Christian bookstore and purchase several gift Bibles. Offer to give a gift Bible to guests or needy families. Let your preschooler participate by asking if guests have a Bible, and giving a Bible to someone who needs one. Say: The Bible is about God. We are giving others a way to learn about God.

Spare Change Bank

Rinse an empty paper half-gallon milk carton with bleach water and let it dry. Cover the sides with construction paper. Ask your preschooler to decorate it with markers, and glue on faces of babies, children, and adults cut from magazines. Close the top, leaving the spout open as if pouring milk. Place the bank near an entry or high-use area of your home. Encourage family members to drop spare change and money into the milk carton bank. Say: Let's save our spare change and give it to somebody who needs it. Who can we help by giving them money?

Choose a church program or charity to give saved change to. Remind your family that giving money is one way to serve others—being a missionary and helping others.

Greeting Card Stockings

Work together with another family to make greeting card stockings and give them to children who have to be hospitalized over the holidays. Call a local hospital and ask how many children are expected to stay during the Christmas holiday.

Materials: Christmas greeting cards, scissors, hole punch, yarn, masking tape, candy canes, small boxes of crayons, small notepads, stickers, permanent marker

Ask family members to form an assembly line. Let oldest members cut a stocking shape from each card (keep the back of the card attached to the front to form a stocking) and punch holes around the bottom edges of each stocking. Help younger family members use yarn to sew the stocking edges together, leaving long pieces at each end. Form a loop with yarn ends and tie a knot. Ask older children to print a holiday message on back of each stocking. Preschoolers can place a candy cane, crayons, stickers, and notepad in each stocking.

Travel to the hospital and give stockings to children in the pediatric wing. Talk to the patients, and say: Merry Christmas! Jesus was born in Bethlehem! Jesus loves you! Get well soon!

Sing Christmas carols while delivering the stockings.

Hint: Wrap masking tape around end of yarn to form a needle.

Tip: Stop at the nurse's station before delivering stockings. Ask permission to visit individual rooms.

WorldCrafts

If you like to purchase gifts and help others at the same time, go to www.WorldCraftsVillage.com. Shop online with your preschooler for a gift for grandparents or teachers. Order a catalog by calling 1-800-968-7301. WorldCrafts purchases gift items made by families living in countries around the world. The income from craft items provides a livelihood for families that need help.

6

Doing

Read More About It: Romans 12:6; 1 Corinthians 3:9; 2 Corinthians 5:9; Colossians 1:10–11

Bible Thoughts for Preschoolers

Jesus went about doing good (see Acts 10:38).

We work together (see 1 Cor. 3:9).

What is doing?

Doing is the physical act of showing love to others. Doing involves others, recipients of acts of kindness, giving, loving, and sharing. Doing is serving others—being a missionary to others. A missionary serves (helps) others and tells about Jesus in the process. All believers in Jesus Christ are missionaries!

This is the part of missions where preschoolers shine! They love doing! As a parent, I'm sure you've noticed that preschoolers *have* to move. You have seen your preschooler move. Preschoolers don't sit still; they go from one thing to the next. They have to learn by doing things, by jumping in the middle of things and getting their fingers right in the center of the action! Doing is our chance to show our love for others and our willingness to serve one another. By letting our preschoolers be involved in doing for others, we are taking advantage of the fact that they learn by doing! We are using their natural way of learning for a big impact.

Why is doing important?

Doing is the outward show of our relationship with Jesus. Doing is service to other families and individuals. When we do things for others, we put our beliefs into action. Many times, people will not hear what we say, but they will see what we do. Our actions tell a story about what and who we believe in.

The Bible tells us to show our love, not just in words, but in deeds (1 John 3:18). We are instruments for God to use to care for each other. When the unsaved see our love and caring in action, they will be drawn to the Savior. God also uses us to take care of and provide for the needs and answer the prayers of other believers. Doing is the visible presence of God in a world that is searching for something. Our part is to help the world see that God is the answer to the questions.

How can I teach my preschooler to do?

Preschoolers love to do! Often, they want to help us more than we want! Realize that their excitement and zest for adventure works perfectly with doing for others.

To teach your child how to do for others, involve them in the decision-making process and discussion of what projects to undertake. Ask your preschooler what he thinks, what activity he would choose, and what the best way to implement that action is. Simplify projects to the level of your child, or change the activity to fit your circumstances. Talk about why you believe that doing for others is important. Share what the Bible says about doing for other families. Practice doing at home. Perform chores, help each other clean a room, pick up toys, or make a bed. Let your child experience doing for family members. When the time comes to take part and do a project for others outside of the family, your child will be ready to do as much as he can! Help with the tough stuff, and be on hand to offer assistance, but let your child push himself and try something new. Work side by side, and talk about the project and what it means to Jesus when we do things for others.

When we allow our preschoolers to do things, to participate in the action, we give them ownership in the process. Each child will grow to understand that he can serve others. Preschoolers will see that they are capable of being a missionary—one who serves other people and tells them about Jesus!

Activities

Doing at Home

Do household chores together. Teach your preschooler how to help by working together. Preschoolers can learn to make a bed, pick up toys, dust, arrange pillows, set the table, help wash dishes, help prepare meals, feed and water pets, put away groceries, and many other household jobs. Use the home as training ground for going out and doing for others!

Make a game of household chores. Take photos of each chore your child can learn to do, such as a picture of the dog, a bed, the dinner table, the mailbox, the toy box, or bookcase. Attach photos to index cards with double-sided tape. Spread the job cards on the table and let your preschooler choose which one she wants to do first. Attach two envelopes to a bulletin board, one marked *Start* and the other marked *Done*. After a chore is complete, teach your child to put the photo card in the *Done* envelope. Keep unfinished job cards in the *Start* envelope. Say: You are learning to do things to help our family! Jesus said to help one another, and you are helping!

Open the Bible, and read: Serve one another (see Gal. 5:13).

Stuffed Animal Collection

Help your preschooler clean out his stuffed animal collection. Ask your child to choose animals that he is willing to give to others. Place them in a box. Shop together at thrift stores and yard sales, and purchase gently used stuffed animals. Clean them, and place in the collection box. When the box is full, go together to a local emergency agency, such as the fire department, police station, or hospital. Donate the stuffed animals. Say: We are doing something for other boys and girls. When they are scared or hurt, they will get a stuffed animal! That will help them not be as scared.

Tip: Call the local agency before collecting stuffed animals. Ask for donation guidelines.

Fast-Food Restaurant Friends

Talk about making friends with your child. Discuss ways to help others at a restaurant.

Eat lunch at a local fast-food restaurant that has a child play area. Pray before eating your meal. Work together to clean up your table and any other trash left around your table. Encourage your preschooler to play and make friends. Visit with other waiting parents. Interact with both preschoolers and adults. If you notice a relationship that clicks, suggest meeting again for lunch—same time, same place. Build a friendly relationship. Tell about and invite your new friends to church services or a special church function.

On the way home, say: I had fun making new friends. Let's pray that we can tell our new friends about Jesus.

Make a Play Dough Kit

Collect cookie cutters, rolling pins (or thick wooden dowels), and vinyl place mats. Make play dough (recipe follows), allowing your preschooler to pour ingredients into the bowl. Let him watch as you pour the boiling water and knead the dough. After the dough is cool, let your child divide it in half. Put half in a plastic container with a lid and place it in a sack. Add a few cookie cutters, a place mat, a roller, and the recipe. Place remaining play dough in a container for your child.

Go with your preschooler to deliver the play dough kit to an ill child or an unchurched friend of your preschooler. Visit with the preschooler and his family. Offer prayer and invite them to church.

PLAY DOUGH

3 cups flour	**1 cup salt**
1 tablespoon alum	**3 cups boiling water**
2 tablespoons baby oil	**Food coloring**

Place flour, alum, oil, and salt in a bowl. Put food coloring in measuring cup and add boiling water. Add boiling water to the bowl. Stir. Cool slightly and dump out onto a counter. Knead well. Store in a covered plastic container.

Flashlight Walk

Give each family member a flashlight. After dark, go on a flashlight walk. Say sentence prayers aloud for the families that you see inside their homes. Invite family members to take turns saying sentence prayers. Say: We are doing something for others. We are praying that these families will love Jesus like we do!

Brownie Sundaes

Before Sunday, shop with your preschooler for ingredients for brownie sundaes. Purchase a brownie mix (or ingredients to make them from scratch), ice cream, chocolate syrup, and whipped cream. Together, follow the directions and make the brownies.

After church services, let your preschooler invite a new family over for dessert. Ask your child to help assemble the brownie sundaes. Put a brownie in a bowl, add a scoop of ice cream, pour chocolate sauce over the ice cream, and put whipped cream on top. Your preschooler can deliver the sundaes, napkins, and spoons to the guests. Before everyone digs in, say a prayer, thanking God for new friends. Enjoy the time of fellowship and dessert! Hint: Build sandwiches before dessert. Or make a second date with your new friends for sandwiches.

Good Friends Bible Club

Begin a monthly Good Friends Bible Club at your house. Ask your preschooler to help plan and prepare for the club. Invite neighborhood preschoolers and their parents. Set a time frame and plan a simple Bible story, a craft, a game, a song, and a snack. Let your child help prepare what is needed for the Bible club. Gather all materials before preschoolers arrive. (See p. 153 for sample plan.)

Enjoy the time telling about Jesus. Encourage your preschooler to make friends. After the friends leave, say: You did a great job making new friends. We can tell our friends about Jesus!

Tip: Involve other parents in gathering materials for future Bible club meetings. Invite them to plan a meeting.

Jesus Loves You Phone Call

Pretend to make phone calls with your preschooler. Use toy phones and talk back and forth. During the phone call, say: Jesus loves you!

Ask your child to think of a friend or person who needs to hear about Jesus. Help dial the number and let your child have a conversation with that person. Encourage your preschooler to tell the person that Jesus loves them.

Caution: For safety purposes, remove toy phone cords.

Paint Over Graffiti

Older preschoolers will enjoy painting over graffiti in your neighborhood. In advance, ask permission from property owners to paint over graffiti. Offer to supply the labor, if they supply the paint. Set a date, gather paintbrushes, and show up in old paint clothes. Show your preschooler how to dip a brush in the paint, wipe off the excess, and paint over the graffiti. Work side by side with your preschooler. Say: We are serving others when we paint over this graffiti. Jesus wants us to help others.

Babies and toddlers will enjoy being a part of the action by watching and being present.

Build a relationship with the home or property owners. Look for a chance to talk about Jesus or invite them to church.

Flowers and Bees

Walk with your child and find a bunch of flowers. Sit near them and watch the busy bees as they zoom from flower to flower. Help your child see what the bees are doing. Explain how bees work together to collect nectar from flowers, and then take it back to the hive to make honey. Say: It takes all of the bees working together to make honey. God wants us to work together like bees and tell others about Jesus.

Jesus Loves You Eggs

Materials: hard-boiled eggs; egg dye kit, prepared according to package directions; cups; spoons or tongs; newspapers; crayons

Cover your work surface with newspapers. Put cups of dye, eggs, crayons, and spoons on the newspapers. Before your preschooler dyes eggs, use a crayon to write *Jesus Loves You* on each egg. Allow your child to draw additional designs on the eggs. Show how to dip the eggs in the dye. Look at the revealed messages! Read them together. Say: We celebrate Easter because of Jesus! We can share these eggs with friends, and let them know that Jesus loves them too!

Store decorated eggs in the refrigerator until you and your preschooler eat them, or give them to neighbors, friends, or family members.

Tip: Invite friends of your child to help decorate eggs. Use the opportunity to have your preschooler talk about Jesus. Send eggs home with each child.

Tissue Box Game

Stuff fabric handkerchiefs into an empty tissue box. Play a game with your baby or toddler. Show your child how to pull a handkerchief from the box. Play peekaboo, and give the handkerchief to your child. Let him pull out a handkerchief and play peekaboo. Encourage him to give you a handkerchief. Take turns pulling out handkerchiefs. Let your child play this giving and sharing game. Say: Thank you for giving me a handkerchief. Thank you for sharing with me. Jesus wants us to give and share.

Family and Friends Game Night

Invite a family with preschoolers from church or your neighborhood to come over for a game night. Ask your preschooler to help you prepare simple snacks, such as peanut butter and jelly sandwiches, juice boxes, cookies, and coffee or tea for the adults. Gather games that are appropriate for the age of your preschooler. Select easy board games, like Candy Land and Twister, as well as movement games, like a beach ball catch, "hide-and-seek," and so on. Enlist one of the adults to prepare a short devotional that includes prayer for the fellowship and the food. Tell your preschooler that Jesus loves people, and He wants us to love people. Say: When we spend time with our friends, we are loving people and having fun!

Play games and have a great time. Consider having a monthly game night. Use the game night as an opportunity to tell families about Jesus and invite them to your church.

Self-Portrait on the Sidewalk

Draw on the sidewalk or driveway with large sticks of chalk (available at toy or craft stores). Let your preschooler scribble away on the cement. Have her lie down while you trace her body. Let her stand up and add details like eyes and hair. Draw a large heart, and print: *Jesus loves you!* next to her outline. Say: Jesus loves you. He loves me. He wants us to tell others that He loves them.

Invite interested preschoolers or children to draw with you. Talk about Jesus as everyone enjoys chalk drawing.

For More Fun: Provide a spray bottle filled with water. Watch what happens when a drawing is sprayed with water.

Homeless Shelter First-Aid Supplies

Play first aid and doctor with your preschooler. Use play doctor toys and a telephone. Take turns being the patient or the doctor. Call people who are sick and tell them how to get well (pretend!). Allow your child to stick an adhesive bandage on a pretend injury. Say: Thank You, God, that we have bandages and things to help us get better.

Talk with your preschooler about homeless people that may not have medical supplies to help them get well. Call a local homeless shelter and ask if they have any first-aid supply needs. Make a list of first-aid needs (adhesive bandages, first-aid cream, tape, aspirin, gauze, etc.). Let your preschooler stick a bandage on the top of the list as a reminder. Shop together for the items, and deliver them to the shelter. Say: We are helping people who don't have a home. We are doing things to help others, just like Jesus wants us to do.

Star Ornaments

Materials: large star cookie cutter, cardboard, marker, scissors, yellow acrylic paint, paintbrushes, glitter, fine-tip permanent marker, hole punch, yarn

Use the cookie cutter to trace star shapes on the cardboard. Cut out star shapes. Let your preschooler paint the stars with yellow paint, and sprinkle glitter on the stars while the paint is still wet. Dry the stars, punch a hole in the top, and make a loop with yarn for hanging. On the back, print *Jesus was born in Bethlehem*. Ask your preschooler to hang some of the ornaments on your Christmas tree. Use some of the stars as package decorations. Encourage your child to tell others the true reason for Christmas.

Tip: Contain glitter by placing wet stars inside a box. Let your child sprinkle the glitter into the box onto the wet paint. Shake off excess glitter into the box.

Bible Thought Door Hangers

Copy the Door Hanger Pattern on page 155. Trace and cut several door hangers from cardstock or old manila folders. Let your child decorate one side of the door hangers with markers. On the other side of each hanger, print a Bible thought from this book. Print greetings below the Bible thought. Include a short invitation to drop in for iced tea. With your preschooler, walk around the neighborhood and place door hangers on each door. Visit with neighbors you see.

Open your porch and home to your neighbors. Let your child welcome guests and give each a drink. Provide cold juice for preschoolers. Get to know your neighbors. Offer to pray for special needs that may be shared. Building a relationship is the first step in being able to tell about Jesus.

For preschoolers and children: Inflate beach balls and provide an empty wading pool. Let your child invite other children to play with the balls and throw them in the pool.

Missing You!

When you pick up your child from Sunday School, day care, or preschool, ask your preschooler who was absent that day. Get permission and contact information from the teacher to contact the missing child. Talk about the possibilities of why people are absent. When you arrive at home, help your child call or draw a picture for the absent friend. Talk on the phone, or mail the picture. Help your preschooler say a sentence prayer for his friend. Say: You are showing your friend that you care about him.

Clothesline of Remembrance

As your family participates in activities that show serving, helping, or doing for others, take pictures. Hang a length of rope on a wall in your home. Allow your preschooler to hang the pictures of servant activities on the rope with clothespins. Look at the pictures and remember the good times the family experienced. Use the pictures as ideas for choosing another activity or as a way to repeat a favorite project. Ask your child to tell what her favorite part of each activity was. Use her answers to plan future activities or projects.

Do Something Nice for People Who Help You

Do you have workers come to your home or apartment building to perform jobs for you (yard worker, plumber, repair person, etc.)? With your preschooler, prepare a glass of iced tea or hot coffee and a muffin. Let your child give the snack and tell the helper thank you. Say: We appreciate your work. Thank you!

Barefoot Walk

Walk barefoot with your child in the wet grass or muddy puddles after a rain shower. Explore the textures with your toes. Enjoy the experience. When you go into the house, wash your child's feet. Say: I enjoy doing this for you. I love you!

If your child is old enough, let him wash your feet! Say: Thank you for washing my feet! You helped me. You are a good helper!

What Did Jesus Do?

Ask you preschooler to help you think of things that Jesus did to help others. Look at a children's book that tells stories about Jesus. On a piece of paper, make a list of things He did to help others. Make it a game to think of as many ways as possible to help or serve others. Write down all ideas from your child, even if they don't make sense! Part of the fun of brainstorming is listing things without having to decide if they will work or not. Keep the list on the refrigerator or in a handy spot.

When your family needs an idea for helping others, look at the list and choose something that appeals to everyone. Adjust the idea to fit your family, your time, and your resources. Away you go, serving others!

7
Helping

Read More About It: Proverbs 22:6; Mark 10:43–45; Galatians 6:9–10; Philippians 2:14–16

Bible Thoughts for Preschoolers

We are helpers (see 2 Cor. 1:24).
Serve one another (see Gal. 5:13).

What is helping?

Helping is to aid or assist another person. To help is to offer assistance, willingly and joyfully. A helpful individual is one who looks for opportunities to help others and jumps at the chance to help! Helpful people rise to the occasion, whatever the need, the situation, or the circumstance.

Offering help requires a willing attitude, time, energy, and loving heart. Reaching out a helping hand helps ease the burdens of others. Offering help is a way to encourage others to keep going. Think about a time when someone has helped you, perhaps with a small task, like holding a door open when your arms were full. Or maybe someone volunteered to help you do something big, such as painting your house! How did you feel? Appreciative, encouraged, joyful, pleased, humbled, perhaps more willing to be thankful for the human race.

Helping others is our chance to be Jesus for someone else. Many people are desperate for a loving hand, a kind smile, extra fingers, a strong back, or unreserved energy. By willingly helping another person, we are showing the love and care of Jesus. One helpful act may be the only nice thing that happens in the day of another person.

Why is helping important?

The Bible is important in teaching us how to live. The Bible tells us to help one another. We are told to help each other, but the details are left wide open. We are even told who to help—everyone! We are instructed to help our neighbors. Our neighbors are fellow human beings (Luke 10:25–37), any and all people.

Jesus was in the business of helping people. His entire purpose was to help us reach God: to provide a way for us to be forgiven of our sins, communicate with the Father, and spend eternity in heaven with Him. During His ministry, Jesus helped many people. He helped them with not just their spiritual needs but also their physical and emotional needs. Jesus realized that meeting the needs of and helping others was vital to spreading the gospel. Helping opens the door to opportunities to tell others about Jesus. Ministering to other people without the expectation of return assistance is a wonderful way to be like Jesus to those who do not know Him. Helping other believers is just as important and leads to the strengthening of our Christian family.

How can I teach my preschooler to help?

Preschoolers love to help! Some days you can hardly get anything done because your child wants to help so much! As a parent, you are in the perfect setting to teach your child about helping. The best place to start is to practice helping each other at home. With unending chores and regular tasks that need completing, home is not only the best place to begin but it is full of ways to help. Home is important to preschoolers. Your child is interested in his home and in exploring and learning all he can about his home. The best way to teach your preschooler *anything* is to begin with something he is already interested in.

Let your child help at home. Give him jobs that he is capable of doing. Break chores into simple steps, and show how to perform each task. Keep in mind that your child is a preschooler, so mistakes will be made and perfection (adult standards) should not be the guideline for your child. Praise your child as he helps, offer help if he needs it, but accept his work without going along behind him and fixing things the way you want them. Avoid criticism, and notice the things that are well done. Practice makes perfect, and your preschooler will improve by repeating tasks.

Teach helpful actions while out in the community. Offer help to others at the grocery store or other shopping areas. Help clear the table when your family eats out at a restaurant. Pick up trash that the wind has blown into the church parking lot. Give a cold soda to a hot worker. Look for ways to assist others, keeping in mind that your child is watching your actions and your attitude!

Activities

Habit of Helpfulness

Cultivate the habit of helpfulness in yourself and your child. Make heart-shaped reminders from construction paper. On each, print *Help one person today*! Let your child place the hearts around your home as reminders to help others.

Each day, with your preschooler, help one other person that is not a family member. Encourage your child to keep looking for ways to help others. If both of you are looking, you will be ready to offer a hand of helpfulness. Watch for the opportunity to help carry a bag of groceries, return a shopping cart to the storage area, pick up a dropped item, or hold a door open. With practice, helpfulness will become a habit for you and your child!

Extra Practice: Role play ways to help others. Pretend to be at the store, library, park, or walking down the sidewalk. Act out ways to help others, including smiling and chatting with the person being helped. Say: We're practicing helping others. Now we'll be ready when we see someone who needs help.

I Spy Someone Who Needs Help

Look around for someone to help. Say: I spy a child who lost a ball over a tall fence. How can we help him?

Let your child say ways to help. Look for other people and situations that need help. Part of helping is being able to notice that help is needed! You may not be able to help every person or situation, but you will become tuned in to notice needs of others.

Soup Kitchen

Make pretend soup with your child. Help her use toy vegetables and food items to make the soup. Let her use a soup pan and a wooden spoon from the kitchen. As she stirs, say: You are making soup. Some people help others by making real soup. They give the soup to hungry people.

Optional: Volunteer at a local soup kitchen or feeding program. Ask if your older preschooler can help serve a meal. If preschoolers are not allowed, ask if the program has any food needs. Help by letting your child donate food items to the program.

Unload the Groceries

Purchasing and putting away groceries is much more enjoyable when help is offered. Ask your child to unpack cans and stack them in the pantry, place the yogurt in the refrigerator, or put the toilet paper in the bathroom. Younger preschoolers can easily perform small tasks, even if it's just emptying sacks onto the floor. Older preschoolers can help organize foods that go into the pantry, the refrigerator, the freezer, or other parts of the home.

Say: Thank you for helping me! Jesus wants us to help each other. Caution: Keep plastic shopping bags away from younger preschoolers.

Coupon Clippers

Teach your preschooler to be a coupon sleuth! Show her what coupons look like in newspaper, magazines, and advertisements. Let her cut them out with child-safe scissors. Together, sort the coupons into like categories, such as milk products, cereals, canned goods, and so on. Let your child hold the coupons as you shop, and help you locate the items for the coupons. Shopping is a great time to ask your child to choose food items, place food into the cart, and help push the cart. Explain why coupons help your family. Say: Using these coupons will save money for our family. Thank you for helping us to save money.

Show your child the receipt, and tell her how much money was saved. If your family is saving money for a special church offering, trip, or project, save the money from the amount of the coupons for the project.

More Ideas to Help Others:

Organize a coupon exchange at church or in your neighborhood. Ask other families to bring clipped coupons. Allow families to trade coupons for ones they will use.

Save coupons and give them to a family that needs extra help making ends meet. Collect coupons that you know other families can use. Your child will develop super eyesight for spotting coupons.

Ask permission from a store manager, and tape coupons on appropriate containers in the store. Your preschooler will enjoy locating the correct item and taping the coupon on the package.

Rake the Leaves

Turn this fall activity into a time of helping. Purchase child-size yard tools (rake and wheelbarrow) at a hardware store. Teach your preschooler how to use the rake to collect leaves. Show how to scoop up the leaves and place them in the wheelbarrow. Let your child enjoy wheeling the leaves and dumping them into a pile. Add the leaves to your compost pile, or bag them for yard waste recycling. Work together to clean your yard!

Help someone in your neighborhood. Take a walk and look for a yard that needs raking. Offer to rake the leaves for your neighbor. Ask your child to help. Say: We are helping our neighbor. How do you think that will make him feel?

Idea: Help an elderly neighbor by shoveling snow in the winter. Provide a child-size snow shovel. Bundle up and enjoy the time spent helping others.

Toy Hunt

Play with your preschooler and her favorite toys. Help her use her imagination and creativity to make up conversations or scenarios with the toys. When you are done playing, help your child put away her toys by making cleanup time into a toy hunt game. Say: Let's play toy hunt. Help me hunt for a toy that has fluffy purple fur.

Locate the described toy and put it away. Let your child give clues for the next toy hunt item. Help her locate and put the toy away. Continue taking turns until the toys are put in their storage places.

Musical Cleanup

Turn family chore time into family fun time! As a family, survey the home to see which tasks need completing. Set a timer for 15 minutes. Play lively music and work as quickly as you can to tidy the house. Race to finish the chores before the timer dings. As soon as the timer goes off, stop, look at the progress that was made, and tell family members thank you for helping. Celebrate by playing a simple board game or reading a favorite story book.

Some chores that can be finished in 15 minutes: vacuum, make the beds, put away toys, gather the dirty laundry, load the dishwasher, dust bookshelves, clear the dinner table.

Will Work for Food

Materials: nonperishable food and drink items, plastic shopping bags, construction-paper hearts that say *Jesus loves you!*

Talk with family members about homeless or jobless people. Discuss the types of food people need. Make a list of nonperishable food and drink items that would help a hungry person. Some items are: bottled water, juice, packaged snack items, chips, crackers, trail mix, raisins, nuts, and energy bars. Shop with your family for the items on your list.

Make food kits with your family. Let each person put one of each item in a plastic shopping bag. Include a *Jesus loves you!* paper heart in each bag. Tie bag handles into a loose knot, and place the bags in a basket or box. Keep the basket in the car trunk. Each time you run errands, place one food bag on the seat beside you or your child. As you drive around your neighborhood or city, watch for hungry people. If you see one, offer a bag of food items. Tell the person "God Bless you!" or "Jesus loves you!" To your child, say: We helped that person have food to eat. Jesus wants us to help other people.

Make Muffins

Ask your preschooler to help make muffins for breakfast. Individually wrap a muffin (or two) in plastic wrap. Deliver one to your pastor or other church worker. Thank your pastor for helping others hear about Jesus. As you leave, say: Our pastor helps us learn about Jesus. We helped him by giving him a yummy muffin for a snack!

PINEAPPLE BRAN MUFFINS

1 egg	1/4 teaspoon salt
3/4 cup milk	1/2 cup crushed wheat flake cereal
1/2 cup oil	
2 cups flour	1/4 cup ground flax seed
1/3 cup sugar	1/2 cup crushed pineapple
1 tablespoon baking powder	1 teaspoon cinnamon

Heat the oven to 400°F. Let your child put muffin papers in a muffin pan. Guide your preschooler as he helps measure and stir the listed ingredients.

Gently stir ingredients together. Spoon batter into muffin papers, filling each about two-thirds full. Bake 15 to 20 minutes, until golden brown. Remove from pan and cool on cake rack. Serve with margarine and jam.

Window Washer

Preschoolers love spray bottles! Pour 1/4 cup of white vinegar into a small spray bottle. Fill the remainder of the bottle with water. Use black and white newspaper pages as drying towels. Let your preschooler spray the cleaning solution on windows and mirrors, and then help dry them off with crumpled newspaper. Help each other make the glass sparkling clean. Say: Thank you for helping me wash the windows.

Take a Helping Walk

Go for a walk with your child. If your preschooler is a baby, carry him in a front pack. Point to and wave at people you see as you walk. Help your baby wave at neighbors and people you know. Show your baby that people are wonderful, and say: Jesus loves all the people. Jesus loves you.

If your preschooler is older, let him or her walk beside you. Help push your child's doll stroller or pull a wagon. Watch for people to help. Encourage your child to wave and say hello to neighbors. Say: Jesus loves all people. He loves our neighbors. He loves you. Jesus wants us to help each other.

Use the wagon or stroller to carry a toy. Or, carry a garbage bag and collect trash as you walk.

Photo Prayer Wreath

Materials: purchased grapevine wreath, colorful ribbon cut into 18-inch lengths, felt heart shapes, clothespins, hot glue gun, photos of people important to your family

Ask your preschooler to help tie ribbons on the wreath. Let him spread the heart shapes around the wreath, and you glue them in place with the glue gun. Attach one ribbon loop to the back of the wreath for hanging. Use the clothespins to clip the photos onto the hearts. Hang the wreath.

Stand in front of the wreath with your child. Hold her up so she can name the people in the pictures. Say sentence prayers for each person. Say: We help others when we pray for them.

Add photos of new friends or missionaries. Pray for others, reminding your child that a missionary is someone who loves Jesus and tells others that Jesus loves them. Say: When we tell someone that Jesus loves them, we are being a missionary!

Cover Up, Uncover Game

Play this game with your baby. Place a favorite toy on the floor. Cover the toy with a hand towel. Help your baby uncover the toy. Help cover it again. Let your baby play the game. After a few turns, change the toy, or cover your face, and play peekaboo with the towel. Say: I'll help you cover the toy. You can help me cover my face. We can help each other.

Play the game with an older preschooler by placing several toys under a towel. Let her peek at the toys, and cover them up again. Help your child think of the things she saw beneath the towel. Check to see if she remembered everything. Play again.

Hug Fest

Create a new game at your house! Teach family members that each time someone says "Hug Fest," it's time to see who can give the most hugs! Drop everything and race to see who gets and who gives the most hugs! Let your child have turns saying "Hug Fest." Tell your family that whenever anyone needs a hug, or is feeling down and needs encouragement, they should yell "Hug Fest!" This game will catch on quick, and your family may spend more time hugging than arguing or complaining. Say: Hug Fest makes me feel better. It helps me when we have a Hug Fest.

Suggest that your child tell a friend about Hug Fest. Play this game at family get-togethers, reunions, or church social activities. Help others feel good by sharing hugs.

Drive-Through Heart Notes

Materials: construction paper, child-safe scissors, markers, plastic bag, dark-colored permanent marker

Spend an afternoon or evening making heart notes. Show your older preschooler how to draw a heart shape. Help your younger child draw heart shapes and hold the scissors to cut out shapes. Decorate lots of shapes. As your child decorates heart shapes, print *Jesus loves you*! on one side of each heart. On the other side, print *We love you*! Place the completed hearts in the bag and put the bag in your car. Say: We will give these hearts to window workers. We will help them feel happy. They will hear that Jesus loves them!

Anytime you go through a drive-through, such as a bank, fast-food restaurant, or coffee stand, surprise the window worker by giving a heart note. Let your child be in charge of reminding you about the hearts, and handing you one to place in the window drawer or give to the worker. Smile and give pleasant greetings.

Help the Animals

Drink cold water with your child. Talk about the importance of fresh water. Ask your child to name some people and animals that need water every day.

With your child, place a birdbath or low-sided container in your garden or yard. Let your child be in charge of keeping it filled with water. Change the water every day. Wash the container weekly. Say: You are helping the birds and animals by giving them water to drink. God gives us good water to drink.

Tip: Place the water container near bushes or plants, so birds will have easy access to hiding places. Place the container in front of a window so your child can enjoy watching birds as they bathe or drink the water.

Adopt a Family

During the holidays, or any other time of year, adopt a family that needs extra help. Ask at church or your child's day care or preschool for the name of a family. Gather a list of needs. With your preschooler, shop for items on the list. Box items and prepare them for delivery. If the family or the needs are large, ask another family to join you and help provide for the needs of the family.

Build a relationship with the family. Explain that you are helping them because Jesus has helped your family, and you want to share the blessings He has given to your family. Pray for the new family when your family has prayertime.

Tip: Depending on the circumstances of the family you are help-ing, decide how to deliver needed items. Ask the person who gave you the family's name the best way to help the family. Some fami-lies in need may be embarrassed or prefer to deal with a teacher or pastor.

Bible Thoughts Computer Banner

Look up the Bible thoughts for this chapter. Using your computer, print a large banner of each Bible thought. Assist your older preschooler in making the banner by letting him locate and punch the letters on the keyboard. Younger preschoolers can decorate the banners with markers or crayons. Hang the banners in the kitchen or dining room area of your home. Point to each word as you read the Bible thoughts with your child. Read them often, reminding family members that the Bible says to help each other.

Outgrown Clothes—Again!

Preschoolers grow fast, sometimes seemingly overnight! Save outgrown clothes in a box. Teach your child to notice when clothes are too tight, too short, or too little. Say: Oops, you grew again! Let's put this in the box for too small clothes! Look at yourself in the mirror. Look at how big you are getting!

Let your child put outgrown clothes in the box. Periodically check the box. Your child might have so much fun putting clothes in the box that she might also put some extra things in it! Look at church or in your neighborhood for a family with children younger than yours. Give them the clothes that your child has outgrown.

Idea: Start a clothing swap with families that have children. Ask families from your church, neighborhood, or day care to join the swap. Instruct each to bring clean clothes to a large room with lots of tables. Allow each family to select the same number of clothing items as they brought. If clothing is left over, donate the items to a local women and children's shelter or another organization that helps families.

What Can I Do? Ask to Help in Your Community

Ask community or church leaders for ways that your family can help. Many newspapers have a volunteer section that lists volunteer needs. Be creative. Volunteer to help people, organizations, or places that are important to your family. Ask your child to help decide where to volunteer or help think of ways to help others.

8

My Friends

Read More About It: Proverbs 17:17; 18:24; John 15:12–17; Ephesians 4:1–6
Bible Thoughts for Preschoolers
A friend loves at all times (see Prov. 17:17).
Jesus said, "You are my friends" (see John 15:14).

What are friends?

A friend is someone that is known, liked, and trusted. A friend is someone who enjoys spending time with us. Friends care for each other, are concerned for each other, and help each other out as needs arise. A friend is someone you think about, reach out to, and want to do special things for.

To have friends, one must be friendly! Friends get along most of the time, but have been known to argue or disagree over certain issues! Part of being a friend, is saying "I'm sorry" and forgiving each other. Friends allow friends to be themselves, even if that means being different.

Friends come in all shapes and sizes. Some friends are closer than others, and some have similar interests or family issues. Some friends are based on a job, the neighborhood school, or neighbors. Some friends are spouses, family members, people recently met, or those who have been in your life since you were small. Friends are a vital and important part of our happiness and contentment as human beings.

Why are friends important?

Friends are important in our lives. Friends provide an anchor when things go wrong or a support when life is stressful. Friends give companionship, encouragement, suggestions, and honest opinions. Most importantly, a friend is someone who can walk beside you in your Christian walk. A good friend makes sure that her friend is a believer. She will seize every opportunity to share the gospel with friends who have not accepted Jesus as Lord and Savior.

The best friend we have as believers is Jesus. He says that He is our friend (John 15:12–17). Wow! The Son of God, the Savior of the world, is our best friend! In our Christian walk, we are constantly learning how to be a friend, both with Jesus and other people.

The more we learn about being a friend, the better we understand how Jesus is our friend. Jesus gives us human friends for three reasons: to learn how to be a friend, to be an encouragement and help to others, and to tell others about the plan of salvation. God's plan is that we share everything with our friends. That includes sharing the story of Jesus. If we have good friends, it only makes sense that we would want to see them in eternity!

How can I teach my preschooler to be a friend?

Parents are just wonderful! They give birth to a tiny package of a baby and immediately begin sharing the baby with everyone! This is the perfect way and time to start teaching a child how to be a friend. The baby is instantly a part of a network of family and friends. As the baby grows, he sees how his parents interact with others. He notices siblings and what they do. He watches other babies while on outings or at church. Even before a baby can talk, he is observing and learning about friends, other people.

As a child grows, parents have the privilege and responsibility of teaching how to be a friend. Use birthday parties, sleepovers, day care or preschool, church, and outings as opportunities to teach friendship skills. Teach your preschooler how to share toys; care for someone who is hurt or crying; say "I'm sorry"; take turns; play together; use polite manners; talk nicely; and use positive physical touch.

A preschooler does not automatically know how to be a friend unless someone explains the ins and outs of friendship. When I was teaching at a preschool, I found that simple, calm statements made a huge impact when teaching social skills. Saying "Friends take care of each other" or "Friends share their toys" was enough to tell or remind a child how a friend should act. As a parent, show and tell your child how to act as a friend. Lectures will not work for young children, but a comment interjected in the midst of play with another child will do wonders. Use everyday experiences and encounters to talk about friendship. Be friends with others, and tell how you do it. Teach your child the importance of telling friends about Jesus!

Activities

Blocks and Cars

Materials: masking tape, wooden blocks, toy cars and trucks, small boxes

Use the masking tape to outline a road on the floor or carpet. Play cars and trucks with your preschooler. Along the road, build homes, stores, and churches with the blocks and boxes. Pretend that friends are going shopping, home, or to church. Say: Friends like to do things together. Jesus is our friend.

Allow your child to invite a friend over to play. Play with them, but also give them time to play with each other. Let your child tell her friend that Jesus is a good friend.

Pets in the Park

Plan a park play date for your child, his friends, their parents, and pets. Print the date, time, and place of the park outing on a strip of paper, and wrap it around a dog bone biscuit. Let your child deliver the invitations. Take treats for both the preschoolers and the pets, such as juice boxes, cookies, and dog bones. Bring along a blanket for snacktime.

Meet at the park. Welcome friends and pets as they arrive. Visit with families and play with the pets. Spread the blanket on the ground, and ask your child to call his friends to come over for a snack. Let him pass out the snacks. Offer a prayer, thanking God for friends and pets.

Pet Show: Bring simple ribbons (see p. 156 for a pattern) for a pet show. Copy the pattern onto brightly colored paper and print a message on each about a pet: *Happiest Doggy Tail, Biggest Dog, Best Dog with Spots,* and so forth. Make one for each child and her pet. Include on each award *Thank You, God, for animals!*

Instruct preschoolers to parade their pets in a circle. Have the parents clap and cheer. Line up the preschoolers and pets, and give each their award. Make sure each child and pet receive an award. Say: Thank You, God, for pets and for friends.

Draw Your Friend

Give your child and her friend paper, markers, and pencils. Guide them to take turns drawing each other (it's OK if neither picture looks like a child!). Give ideas of things to include: eyes, ears, hair, mouth, nose, freckles, and so on. Label pictures with children's names and display them on your refrigerator. Say: Friends have fun together. You are friends.

Friendship Stickers

Preschoolers love stickers. Visit a Christian bookstore or school supply store and let your child choose stickers. When your child sees a friend, encourage him to give a sticker to his friend. Let him explain where he got the stickers and what they mean.

As you go your way, say: A friend likes to give gifts to his friends. You gave your friend a gift.

Let your child invite a friend over to make a sticker book. Provide colored construction paper, markers, and a stapler. Help staple pages together to make a book. Print a Bible thought from this chapter on the front of the book.

Baby's Friends

Include baby in visiting with friends or people you see at restaurants, doctor's offices, or stores. As you sit and wait, hold baby on your lap, facing away from you. Let baby look at the person you are speaking to. If the other person has a baby, let the two babies face each other to make eye contact. Continue with your visit. Introduce your baby to other people, and allow your baby to interact with others. Let your baby watch you talk with others. Tell your baby: Friends love each other. Jesus is our friend.

If you have a toddler, sit on the floor as you wait for appointments. Play with your child and other preschoolers who wander over to where you are sitting. Show your toddler how to interact with other preschoolers. Say: Friends take care of each other.

Allow your older child to interact with other children in the waiting room. If necessary, suggest a way to solve a problem or an idea for what to play. Say: I like the way you are taking turns with the blocks. You are working together.

Cookie Play Date

Let your child invite a friend over for an afternoon of cookie decorating. Before the friend arrives, bake or purchase plain sugar cookies. If you make the cookies, ask your child to help you roll out and cut heart shapes from the dough.

Divide a container of white icing into three bowls. Add a different color of food coloring to each bowl and mix well. Provide shaker containers of sprinkles and cookie decorations, butter knives, plates, damp towels (for wiping sticky fingers), and a cake pan.

Invite the friends to wash hands and decorate cookies. Show how to spread icing. Place the iced cookies in the cake pan and sprinkle decorations on top. Put decorated cookies on a plate.

After the cookies are decorated, share a snack of cookies and milk. Say a sentence prayer: Thank You, God, for friends, and for yummy cookies!

Birthday Party Friends

Use birthday parties to help your child make friends and to help share Jesus. Implement the following ideas into your child's birthday party to practice making friends and sharing the gospel:

- Invite the same number of similar-aged guests as the age of your child (for example, two preschool-age guests if your child is turning two).
- Instead of a cake, bake cupcakes. Turn cupcake decorating into a party activity.
- Plan fun games for interaction and time to practice friendship skills.
- Focus on games that encourage cooperation instead of competition. Play a game where preschoolers see how fast they can work together to fill a container with water, or how far they can place blocks in a domino line (and knock down the line, of course!).
- Pray before eating birthday treats. Thank God for each child by name.
- Make a tradition of the birthday child saying thank you to the giver after each gift is opened.
- Include a Christian trinket, toy, or book in take-home bags for the preschoolers who come to the party.
- Give your child at least one gift that relates to Jesus, God, the Bible, church, or a Christian lifestyle. Tell how the gift will be helpful in learning about God after your child has opened it.

- Take a group photograph of party participants. Make copies. On the back of each, print: *Thank you for coming to my ___ birthday! God loves you!* Let your child print her name. Give one to each child in the picture.
- If your child is invited to a birthday party, shop for a gift at a Christian store.

I Can Pray for My Friends

Encourage your preschooler to pray for her friends during bedtime prayers. Display a birthday group photo or other photos of her friends on a wall or bulletin board near her bed. Teach your child that praying for her friends is a way to love and help them. Say: *Jesus prayed for His friends. He wants us to pray for our friends.*

Bubble Fun

Let your child invite a friend over for outside fun. Prepare bubbles (recipe follows), inflated beach balls, a tub filled with water, empty plastic bottles for play in the tub, and lunch. Show your child and his friend how to blow bubbles, pour and dump water in the tub, and catch and kick the beach ball. As you serve lunch, allow your child to pray for the food. Include your own prayer. Say: Thank You, God, for giving us friends!

BUBBLES

1 cup of dishwashing liquid
1/4 cup light syrup
1 empty plastic gallon milk jug
Water

Pour ingredients into the milk jug. Slowly add water to fill the jug. Let sit overnight.

Pour the bubbles into a plastic tub. Provide bubble wands, plastic rings from packs of canned soda, a plastic colander, and rings cut from plastic lids that came on butter, sour cream, or yogurt tubs. Show how to dip the tools into the bubble mix, and move to make bubbles.

New Baby Bag

Include your child in preparing a welcome bag for a new baby in your child's friend's family. Choose a baby gift bag, and fill it with items for the baby, such as a bib, diapers, diaper wipes, baby soap, shampoo, lotion, and so on. Add homemade cookies for the family members. Include a note that says: *Praying for you! Congratulations!*

After the baby is born, let your preschooler deliver the gift bag. Let your child's friend open the bag. Congratulate the new sibling on being a big brother or sister. Suggest a time for the friend to visit your home, to allow the mom and new baby to rest. Say: You have a new baby. What a wonderful gift from God! Thank You, God, for this baby.

New Baby Banner

Is your child expecting a new sibling? Get your child on the baby bandwagon. Let her help you tape several pieces of construction paper together, end to end, to form a banner. Print large letters that say: *Welcome, Baby!* Use markers to decorate the banner with your child. Give your preschooler child-safe scissors and let her cut long pieces of streamers. Staple the streamers along the sides of the banner. With your child, hang the baby banner above the baby crib. Say: You are going to have a new baby brother or sister! You can be a friend to your new baby.

Beaded Necklace

Purchase red, white, and alphabet beads, and string at a craft store. Measure the string to fit over your child's head, plus enough extra for tying a knot. Show your preschooler how to string the beads in a red-white pattern. In the center of the necklace, string beads that spell *Jesus Loves You* or your child's name.

After the necklace is complete, tie a double knot, and let your child wear it.

Ask your child to think of a friend who needs to know about Jesus. Make another necklace for the friend. Let your child give the necklace to his friend. Say: Friends love each other. Friends tell their friends about Jesus.

Caution: Give beaded necklace to an older preschooler, one who will not eat the beads!

Paint the Fence

Provide your child and a friend a large container of water, small plastic pails, and paintbrushes. Let them enjoy painting a fence with water (or a sidewalk, a brick wall, or another waterproof object). As they paint, say: Friends help each other. Friends work together. Friends have fun!

Bible Thought Bucket

Materials: metal bucket filled with sand, wooden rulers, index cards with Bible thoughts from this book printed on one side, heart rubber stamp, ink pad, tape

Let your child stamp hearts on the back side of the Bible thought index cards. Help your child tape a Bible thought to the top of each ruler. Let her stick rulers into the bucket of sand. Place the bucket beside the front door.

Each time your child has a friend over, let your child invite the guest to choose a Bible thought ruler as he goes home. Read the Bible thought for the young guest, and explain the purpose of the ruler. Say: A ruler is used to measure things. Let's measure a friend.

Use the ruler to measure the friends.

Tip: Purchase rulers during back-to-school supply sales.

Friendship Stew and a Movie

Copy the Friendship Stew and a Movie Invitation on page 157. Fill in the blanks for the time, place, date, and your child's name. Ask your child to give or help mail the invitations to several friends.

On the date of the movie, place a large bowl and small, self-sealing plastic bags on the table. Prepare extra bags of ingredients (cereal rings, pretzels, raisins, or chocolate chips). Chill boxes of juice.

Instruct your child to be the host, and welcome each guest at the door. After the guests have arrived, pass around the bowl, allowing each to dump their stew ingredients inside. Take turns stirring the stew. Fill each bag with friendship stew. Let your child give a bag to each guest. Say: We worked together to make our friendship stew. Friends work together and have fun with each other!

Watch a movie while snacking on the friendship stew and drinking chilled drinks.

Allergy Alert: Always ask parents about food allergies.

Parachute Fun

Materials: large white sheet; permanent markers; newspapers; beach balls or foam balls; Christian music

Let your child invite friends over to make a parachute. In advance, cut a circle-shaped parachute from a large sheet. Spread newspapers on the floor, and place the sheet on top. Show preschoolers how to trace their hands on the sheet and make other designs to decorate the parachute. Play music as the preschoolers work.

When the parachute is finished, take your child and his guests outside. Spread the preschoolers around the perimeter of the parachute and show how to hold the edges tightly with their hands. Drop a ball in the center and let them shake the parachute up and down to bounce the ball. Make up silly games to play with the parachute.

Painting Garden Rocks

Lead this two-session activity with your child's friends at your child's day care, preschool, or Sunday School class.

Materials: large, flat river rocks; old toothbrushes; bar of soap; tub of water; old towels; newspaper; paintbrushes; acrylic paint; glitter in a shaker; acrylic sealer; aprons; paper plates

Session 1: Spread newspapers on a work surface. Guide your child and his friends to choose a rock and use soap and a toothbrush to scrub it clean. Talk about being friends and the things that friends enjoy doing together. Print each child's name on his rock.

Session 2: Spread newspapers on a work surface. Squirt paint onto paper plates. Let the friends paint their rocks. Let each child sprinkle glitter on his rock while it is still wet with paint. Let rocks dry. Ask each child to carry his rock outside, and you spray each rock with acrylic sealer. Dry overnight.

Say: Put these garden rocks in your yard. When you see your rock, you will remember the fun you had with your friends. Thank You, God, for friends.

Spin the Friendship Bottle

Teach your child and her friends a friendship game. Ask them to sit in a circle. Place an empty, clean plastic bottle on the floor in the center of the circle. Show how to spin the bottle. After the bottle stops spinning, say one nice thing about the friend that the bottle is pointing to. Let preschoolers take turns spinning the bottle. Each time the bottle stops, the child who spun the bottle must say a nice comment about the friend on the other end of the bottle. Say: The Bible says that friends love at all times. You show love when you say nice things about your friends.

Feathers in a Sack

Fill a lunch sack with feathers. With your family, sit around the sack. Let each person close her eyes and pull out a feather. As each pulls out a feather, have her name a friend, person, or thing that she is thankful for. After each person has several turns, lead a family prayer, and thank God for giving friends and the things we need.

Play this game with your child and her friends when they have a play date.

Feelings Cup

Print feeling words on pieces of paper (*happy, sad, mad, scared, excited, grumpy, nervous, hungry, loving, surprised*). Fold the pieces of paper and put them in a plastic cup.

Play this game with your child and his friends to teach them to show and recognize feelings. Let one child choose a piece of paper. Open the paper, and whisper the feeling word in his ear. Have him act out the feeling, or make a face that shows the feeling. Ask other preschoolers to guess the feeling word he is showing. After the feeling is guessed, have the preschoolers act out the feeling. Continue with other feelings. Say: God made us with feelings. We can tell our feelings to our friends.

Tip: Play this game with family members. Let family members practice using words to tell about their feelings.

Baseball Golf

Provide two plastic baseball bats and a soft foam ball for your child and a friend. Show how to lay the ball on the grass and take turns hitting it around the yard. Place a cardboard box on its side for older preschoolers to use as a goal. Say: Friends share their toys and take turns when they play.

Make Music with Friends

Materials: toilet paper rolls or paper towel tubes cut in half; masking tape; markers; uncooked rice; spoon

Give your child and a friend paper tubes and let them decorate them with markers. Fold one end together and tape it closed.

Allow each preschooler to pour a spoonful of rice into the tube. Fold and tape the other end closed.

Play lively instrumental music and move to the music with your child and his friend. Shake the tube instruments to the music. Say: God gave us ears to hear music. He gave us friends to enjoy!

9
My Church

Read More About It: Psalm 122:1; Galatians 6:1–6; Ephesians 4:12,15–16; 5:15–21; 1 Thessalonians 5:12–13; 1 Timothy 3:15

Bible Thoughts for Preschoolers

I like to go to church (see Psalm 122:1).
Jesus went to church (see Luke 4:16).

What is church?

Church is a gathering of believers. Church is a time when Christian believers worship the Lord, pray, give, serve, and learn from each other, teachers, and preachers, and encourage and support each other. Church is a time of coming together and seeking fellowship with God and other Christians. Church is for all people: the imperfect, messed-up, seeking-guidance, and needing-help people. Church is for everyone.

Some people think church means a building, the place where people worship. That is one meaning of church. Not every fellowship of believers meets in a church building. There are many types of places that believers meet: store buildings, schools, homes, tents, parks, cathedrals, apartments, and simple-roofed shelters. But in the Bible, Paul talks about the church as being made up of people (Eph. 4–5). To our Father in heaven, the church is the people.

Why is church important?

The Bible tells us to join together with other believers. One major purpose of church is to share in the worship of our God. We were created for His pleasure! Another purpose is to gain support and camaraderie from other Christians. God never intended that we survive on our own as Christians. His plan is that we band together, for the building up and instructing of each other. He wants us to learn from, rely on, serve and help, hold accountable, encourage, and grow together. Going to church is a major part of God's plan for our spiritual development.

Let's pretend that church is our gas station, and we are the vehicles. It is important that we regularly attend church services to get our gas—our spiritual nourishment! If we don't make regular stops, we will soon run out of the energy that keeps us healthy and going strong in our Christian walk. Even if we have a consistent daily devotional time with the Lord, we still need the regular meeting with other believers—full-service deal—gas, oil check, and the windows washed!

God's plan for the church is for the equipping of the saints— that's us, the believers. God wants believers to work together, to train each other, to grow, and to use the spiritual gifts given by God to each believer. He planned for the church, believers working together, to help raise children in a family of Christians. Going to church is the perfect way for you and your child to meet friends who have the same beliefs you do. God wants families to go to church and be a part of His church!

How can I teach my preschoolers to go to church?

The absolute best way to teach your child to go to church is to go to church! The godly habit of weekly, regular worship with a strong body of believers (the church) is established only through practice. Lots of practice! Your child is going to value what you as a parent values. Your child will learn the habits that you practice. If you practice a commitment to a local church group, your preschooler will learn to see commitment and attendance at church as important. If you practice painting red spots on green chairs your child will see that you value painting spots on green chairs, and will soon want to join you painting spots!

If you do not already belong to a church, choose a local church that teaches the Bible. There are many choices available, but most important is that the church keeps the Bible as its ultimate authority and guide. The saving message of the death, burial, and resurrection of Jesus Christ should be a focal point in the beliefs of the church you choose.

Take your preschooler to church with you. Expect all family members to attend services, age-grouped classes, and Bible study groups. Participate in social offerings and get to know people. Bond with the believers, and offer to use your gifts to help the church family. Go to church, rain or shine. Make a commitment to be at church each time the doors open. Become an integrated part of a local church family, and see the impact regular attendance will make on your family.

Activities

Sundays for Church and Family

Keep Sundays for a day of church, family, rest, and fellowship. Commit to attending church and age-grouped classes. Spend the afternoon with family members, enjoying the time of relaxation, games, reading, resting, and playing. Make it a habit to avoid work projects, working at a job, shopping, or running errands on Sundays. Keep the day holy for the Lord. Relaxed family downtime will help everyone be refreshed and ready to go for the busy week ahead. If this habit is started when your child is young, it will become an important part of his life.

Occasionally, your church fellowship will offer a potluck or family outing following services. Please participate in the chance to build friendships and socialize with fellow church family members. At other times, it is a good idea to invite a new family or family friends over for a meal after church. But avoid overscheduling Sunday afternoons. One Sunday afternoon special event a month is enough for a family with preschoolers.

Talk with your preschooler about the choices that you make. Say: Sunday is a special day for going to church and for families. We will learn more about God and spend time together as a family.

Plant a Tree or Shrub

If your church has grounds surrounding the building, volunteer to purchase and plant a decorative tree or shrub. Discuss your idea with the pastor or grounds keeper, and get permission for a location of where to put the new plant.

With your child, visit a garden store. Choose a tree or shrub that will create beauty as it grows. Let your child help select, pay, and cart away the new plant. Take the plant, a shovel, hose or watering can, and a camera to the church. Ask your child to help you dig a hole larger and deeper than the plant pot. Let your preschooler fill the hole with water and let it soak into the ground. Gently remove the plant from the container, loosen the root ball, and lower it into the hole. Assign your child the task of holding the plant upright as you spread soil around the roots. Tamp down the soil. Soak the new plant with water. Take a picture of your child standing beside the plant as a reminder of the size of both when it was planted.

Check on the plant when you go to church. Point out changes and growth to your child. Say: When we planted this tree, we were helping our church look beautiful!

Build a Church

Play with your preschooler and build a church. Use wooden blocks, shoe boxes, masking tape, and paper tubes. Create a structure and tape it in place. Let your child figure out a way to make a cross for the church. After the building is complete, gather toy cars and people. Pretend to drive the cars and people to church. Say: Jesus went to church. We go to church!

Wash the Pastor's Car

Gather a bucket, car soap, large sponges or dishcloths, towels, and access to a water hose.

With your family, sneak to the pastor's office or his home, and wash his car. Wet the car first, and then scrub with soapy water. Let your preschooler help as much as possible. Rinse the car well, and then dry with towels. Clean up your tools, and sneak away. To your child, say: We are going to surprise the pastor! We showed him that we loved him by washing his car! How do you think he will feel?

Tip: Get the OK from your pastor's wife before washing the car.

Greetings Are Important!

Teach your family the importance of greetings. Make it a family habit to greet people as they come into your church. Say hello, learn names, and show families which direction to go for services. Greetings are especially important for visitors or new members to your church family. Encourage your preschooler to say hello to other preschoolers, introduce himself, and ask for the name of his new friend. Say: When we say hello and are nice to people, they know that we love them. It makes them feel welcome at church.

Bible Thought and Church Photo

Ask a church member to take a photo of your family in front of the church. Develop the photo and let your child use a glue stick to attach it to construction paper. Print the Bible thoughts for this chapter beneath the photo. Use magnets to stick the photo poster to your refrigerator. Look at the picture and read the Bible thoughts as you prepare for going to church. Say: Jesus went to church. He wants us to go to church. I like to go to church!

With your child, look up and read the Bible thoughts in your family Bible. Share a few things that you like about going to church. Ask your preschooler to tell why she likes to go to church.

Volunteer!

Sign up to help teach a preschool-age class or serve a rotation in the baby-care room. Show your preschooler that you value his age group, and help with that classroom. Most churches usually have a shortage of volunteers in the baby, toddler, and preschooler classrooms. The most important thing with volunteering is to show up on your assigned day! Follow the lead of the regular teacher. Bring along a cheerful, helpful, happy attitude, and have a great time! The teachers in the preschool classroom will be encouraged as you help out with the preschoolers.

Spring Cleaning

Ask your child's Sunday School teacher if your family could help with spring cleaning of the classroom! Arrange a time to meet with your child's teacher, and plan for supplies that you will need (vacuum, dusting spray and cloth, disinfectant, and so on). Gather supplies with your preschooler and family members. Wear work clothes.

Help the teacher clean. Some tasks that would be helpful are: disinfect toys; dust, sort, and organize block area; wash windows; sort and organize dress-up area; take dress-up clothes home for washing and mending; vacuum carpet or sweep and mop floor; clean and organize craft supplies; work and stack puzzles; organize paper supplies; and dust shelves.

As you complete the work day, thank the teacher for being dedicated to teaching preschoolers about God. Tell your child: We all have jobs to do for God. You helped your teacher. She teaches you about God. Thank you for helping.

Church Hunt

Go for a family drive or walk and look for churches. Play a game to see who can be the first to spy a church as you walk or drive past. Point out the differences in the buildings. Greet people you see around the churches. End by walking or driving past your church. Lead your family in a prayer for the churches that teach about Jesus. Say: Jesus wants us to go to church to learn about Him. He wants us to learn to help, love, and serve each other.

Dessert Social

Invite church families to stop for dessert at a local ice-cream or hamburger shop after an evening service. Let your preschooler invite the family of a friend to meet with you. Get to know other families. Your child will enjoy not only the special dessert but also the chance to play and interact with a friend in a setting that is different from church. Spending time together helps form strong bonds and enriches the family life of church members.

"Follow the Leader"

Play "follow the leader" to teach your child about your church. Ask each family member to be a leader for part of the church tour. Let your preschooler begin the game by leading your family to her classroom. Look in the room and let her tell what the room is for. Choose another leader to lead the family to a different area of the church. Continue, stopping at each room or major feature of your church. Allow your preschooler to tell what she thinks each is for, and then you can add to what she says. Tell that the purpose of the church building is to provide a place for Christians to come and learn about Jesus.

Babies and toddlers will enjoy the tour if you change the way you move as you "follow the leader." Change from little, tiny steps, to bouncing up and down steps, to long, smooth steps, to crawling or hopping (avoid running). Vary the way you move throughout the building, but maintain a respectful attitude while touring the church.

Crayon Melt Greeting Cards

Materials: food warming tray, copier paper, unwrapped crayons, scissors, construction paper, glue sticks, markers, pencil

Plug the warming tray in to heat up. Caution your preschooler about the hot tray. When the tray is warm, lay a piece of copier paper on top. Show your child how to move a crayon around slowly on the paper, causing the crayon to melt. Work with your child to mix melted crayon colors on the paper. When the paper is covered with designs, use the tip of a pencil to lift the paper off of the tray. Let it cool as your preschooler decorates another paper. Unplug the tray.

Cut construction paper in half, and fold each piece to form a card. Cut each crayon melt page into four equal parts. Let your child use a glue stick to attach one piece of paper onto a construction-paper card.

Use these colorful cards to send to church family members. Ask your child to think of a person who needs a card, someone who has been sick or gone. With your child, print a message inside the card that says: *Praying for You*. Sign names, place the card in an envelope, and mail it. Pray for the person who will receive the card. Say: This card will encourage our friend. Our friend will know that we love him.

Big Box Church

Visit a local furniture store and ask for an empty couch or chair box. Take the box home. Make a church with your child. Let your child draw doors and windows on the church. Use a box knife to cut holes for the door and windows. Make the door large enough for your child to fit through. Provide markers to decorate the walls of the church. Draw a large cross on a wall. Put a chair or pillow and a Bible in the church. Go to church with your preschooler! Read the Bible and talk about Jesus. Say: We go to church to learn about Jesus. The Bible tells us about Jesus.

Tip: If the weather is nice, place the church outside. Provide tempera or acrylic paints and let your child paint the church!

Obstacle Course

Organize an outdoor obstacle course. Ask other preschool parents, teachers, and teenagers to help. Create an obstacle course with tires, boxes, hoops, chalk lines to follow, balance beam, a tunnel, a simple jungle gym toy, a slide, a basketball hoop, bubbles, and so on. Create an obstacle using anything that your child would enjoy doing, like climbing, jumping, crawling, sliding, riding a tricycle, bouncing, walking, and running. Create stopping points where each child will have a break. The stopping stations could be to make a snack, pour a drink of water, repeat a Bible thought, say a sentence prayer for a friend, or have a photograph taken. Have a planning meeting with other parents, and agree who will bring what equipment. Encourage parents and preschoolers to invite friends and unchurched families with preschoolers. Let your child call friends on the phone to invite them to the obstacle course day.

Have the obstacle course day on a nice, warm day. Lay out the obstacles in an easy-to-follow path. Place adult helpers at strategic points to assist preschoolers. Enjoy the afternoon of fun!

Tell new families about the preschool classes offered by your church. Invite them to church.

Scavenger Hunt

Invite church families to go on a scavenger hunt. In advance, call a local food bank (or person in charge of your church's food pantry) and ask for specific needs. Print a list of needs, adding a simple sketch of each item for preschoolers who do not read. Copy the list for each family and gather markers.

Give each family a list and a marker. Instruct families that they have one hour to go and gather items on their list and return to church. Tell that preschoolers are to be in charge of the list and need to mark off each item as it is found. Advise families that they can look for needed items at home or at a store.

Set the timer, coordinate watches, and send everyone off on the scavenger hunt. Take your family and find your list of supplies. Let your preschooler be in charge of the list. After the list is checked off, return to the church.

Celebrate with each family as they return to the church. Combine all the resources gathered. Take a group photo of all the families and all the found items. Ask a volunteer to lead a prayer for the ministry and the people who will receive the food. Deliver the food.

Post the photo on a church bulletin board for all the families to see.

Kitchen Aprons

Materials: two plain canvas or cotton aprons, acrylic paint in your child's favorite two colors, two paper plates, permanent marker, newspaper

Spread newspaper on the table and place the aprons flat on top of it. Let your child squirt a small amount of one paint color in a paper plate and the other color in another plate. Stand behind your child and help him dip one hand in a color, making sure the bottom of his hand is covered in paint. Make hand prints on the aprons. Wash hands, and do the same thing with the other color and the other hand, placing hand prints in areas where there is no print. After paint is dry, use the marker to print on each apron *Thank you for serving others!*

With your child, give the aprons to the church hostesses. Say: Thank you for serving us and other families at church.

Holiday Caroling

Plan a churchwide Christmas caroling outing to a local nursing home. In advance, call the nursing home and select a date and time for caroling.

Invite church families to meet at the nursing home. Ask each family to bring individually wrapped candy canes. Bring a large basket and enough bells for each child to have one for ringing as you sing. Ask your child to give each child a bell to ring. Put all candy canes in the basket, and ask a parent to hold the candy canes. Let preschoolers take turns giving a candy cane to residents as you walk the halls and sing. Celebrate Christmas by serving others.

As you go home, say: We served others today. Our church family helped others feel good by singing songs for them and giving them a candy cane.

Pastel-a-thon

Materials: chalk pastels, white construction paper frames, markers, digital or instant camera, tape, markers

Invite church preschoolers and their families to come to a pastel-a-thon. Arrange materials on a table, and let family members decorate a frame with pastels. Along the bottom, print: *Jesus loves you!* Take a photo of each family. Print the pictures and let each family place their photo in the frame.

Church Welcome Bags

Materials: paper bags; individually wrapped candy; index cards printed with *Jesus Loves You*; decorative rubber stamps; ink pad; stapler; marker; flyer printed with church information (address, services, program information)

Let your preschooler decorate the bags with rubber stamps. Print: *Welcome* on each bag. Help your child stuff the bags with the informational flyer and candy. Staple closed. Say: We want other families to come to church. We will give them a bag and invite them to church.

With your child, distribute the welcome bags to your neighbors or to families at a shopping area. Invite them to come to your church. Share about your church if questions are asked.

Church Drawings

Place paper, pencils, markers, and crayons on the kitchen table. Let family members draw pictures of your church. Show your preschooler how to make the outlines of the church and color it in. Draw a cross on top. Talk about the importance of church as you draw. Say: Jesus wants us to go to church. At church we will learn how to be like Jesus.

Prayerwalk Around Your Church

Arrive early for services one day. With your preschooler, take a prayerwalk around your church building. Stop at the corners, and take turns saying sentence prayers. Lead your child to pray for the people who go to church: the preschoolers and their families, the pastor and his family, and the new people who will come to the church. Pray that people will become more like Jesus when they come to church.

10

My Neighborhood

Read More About It: Matthew 22:37–39; John 13:34–35; 2 Corinthians 2:14–15; Ephesians 4:25–32; 5:1–2

Bible Thoughts for Preschoolers

Jesus said, "Love one another" (see John 15:17).
Work with your hands (see 1 Thess. 4:11).

What is a neighborhood?

A neighborhood is the place you live. Many people think of a neighborhood as houses or apartment buildings. But more specifically, a neighborhood is made up of neighbors—people! A neighborhood is made up of people who live near each other, take their kids to the same school, shop in nearby stores, and frequent area businesses, churches, and community offerings. Neighbors are families, single parents, grandparents, people who work outside the home, people who stay at home, people who are single, retired, handicapped, healthy, believers, nonbelievers, and of similar or unfamiliar cultural backgrounds. A neighborhood is a community made up of different people with different backgrounds and different needs.

The song that Mister Rogers sang comes to mind: "Who are the people in my neighborhood? They're the people that you meet each day!" The people we meet each day are our neighbors. The Bible tells of another person who wanted to know "And who is my neighbor?" (Luke 10:25–37). A neighbor is anyone we come into contact with: a person who lives next door, or down the street, or is just traveling through the city we live in. Jesus tells us to love our neighbor as we love ourselves. He doesn't tell us to be nice if we feel like it. He says do it—love our neighbors!

Why is neighborhood important?

As believers in Christ, we are missionaries, called to tell others about Jesus. Our first missions field (the place we tell about Jesus) is our own family. We certainly want to tell and teach them about Jesus! Our neighborhood is our second missions field. We live in the place that God has put us for a reason. He wants us to reach out to our neighbors, to help, love, and care for them. He wants us to tell them about His Son Jesus. We may be the only ones in our neighborhood that know Who Jesus is, or the only ones that live a life that shows Who Jesus is and why He is important.

In the uncertainty and instability of current times, families face fears about many things. Families (neighbors) have fears about the future; having a good job; the high cost of living; the presence of drugs, alcohol, pornography, and violence in the area; the safety of family members; getting a good education; and many other things. You are in a unique position to form a relationship with your neighbors and tell them of the saving hope of Jesus. No one else lives where you do, and no one else has the same opportunities to share about God that you will have.

How can I teach my preschooler to be a neighbor?

Anything we do to make our neighborhood a better place is wonderful. Think about the kind of neighbor you would like to have, and then aim to be that kind of neighbor for your preschooler to learn from. Good neighbors take care of each other, watch out for each other, help and love each other. Neighbors get to know each other, not just names and places of residence, but needs, fears, dreams, and desires. Teach your child to value neighbors as unique individuals and to value the importance of building a relationship with others. Relationships are the basic step in beginning to share about Jesus.

Teach your child to express greetings to neighbors. Get to know your child's friends and their families. Spend time visiting with neighbors at informal gatherings. Get out into the neighborhood and learn about people. Help when you see a need, and let your child help you. Do something good for your neighborhood, and include your entire family in the process. Show by your attitude that the people living around you are important to you, and more importantly, to God. The more you learn about your neighbors, the more you will be able to give a helping hand or a hug, offer a meal, babysit for an emergency, or give a ride to an appointment.

Spend time in your neighborhood with your preschooler. Teach how to interact with others and build relationships. Remember, you are your child's best teacher. When he sees you helping the neighbor with a flat tire, or carrying groceries in for the elderly woman next door, he will learn the value of being a good neighbor.

Activities

Walk and Greet Others in Your Neighborhood

Make a nightly ritual of spending time walking with your child around the neighborhood. Get to know the neighbors. Let your child introduce herself or greet by name the ones she knows. Spend time outside visiting with the people you meet. Share common concerns, child-rearing cares, or community events.

Whatever the age of your child, she will enjoy getting out with her parent. Many people are drawn to a baby or young preschooler. Use your child as a way to begin a conversation with new neighbors or people you haven't met before.

Make a game out of which mode of transportation you use for your nightly walks. Let your child choose which to use each night: wagon, stroller, scooter, or feet. Let her take along a stuffed animal or favorite toy as company and as a conversation starter.

Just Passing By—Waving and Greeting

Make a commitment to wave at and greet neighbors as you drive by on your way to work, school, or to run errands. Encourage your child to wave and notice the families walking, living, and working in your neighborhood. Say: I'm so glad we have neighbors. Jesus said for us to love one another! I love our neighbors.

Welcome Door Sign

Quietly announce to your neighbors that you are a Christian and believe in Jesus. With your child, shop for and purchase a door decoration that says: God Bless You, Jesus Loves You, another Christian saying, or a Bible verse. Let your child help choose the decoration he likes. As you shop, say: We want to tell our neighbors about Jesus. One way we can do that is to have a decoration on our door. When they visit, they will read the sign!

Display the sign on your front door. Help your child read the words. Explain what the words mean.

Play in the Front Yard

Play outside with your child in your front yard. Let your child choose what he would like to play, and play with him. Some fun outdoor activities are: catch with a ball, jump rope, toss a flying disk, balloon bounce, bounce a ball, or drive a remote-control truck. Spend time playing whatever game or activity your child enjoys in the front yard. Be visible to the neighbors around you.

Chat with people who walk by. If they have young children, invite them to come and play for a few minutes.

If you live in an apartment building or far from neighbors, spend time at a local park. Get to know the families you meet.

Decorate Clay Flower Pots

Materials: flat of annual flowers, potting soil, paint brushes, acrylic paint, newspaper, paper plates, clay pot for your preschooler, iced tea and lemonade, plastic cups

Invite the neighbors you have met to come and paint a clay pot and fill it with flowers. Tell each to bring a clay pot they would like to decorate.

Let your preschooler help by spreading newspaper on the ground. Squirt small amounts of paint onto paper plates. Invite your child and neighbors to paint designs on the clay pots. Clean up and share a cool drink while the pots dry. When the pots are dry, let each person fill his pot with soil, and plant a few flowers. Encourage neighbors to display their clay pots so all can enjoy the colorful flowers.

Tell your child: The Bible tells us to work with our hands and love each other. That's what we did today!

Photo Bible Thought Greeting Cards

Materials: photos of your family, either individual or entire group; cardstock, cut in half; glue sticks; scissors; permanent pen; envelopes; markers

With your child, sort family pictures. Let your preschooler choose several pictures of favorite poses or activities. Help your child fold pieces of cardstock in half to form a card. Trim photos to fit, and let him spread glue on the backs and stick them on cards. On the inside, print Bible thoughts from this chapter. Let your child decorate the back of the cards and envelopes with markers. Say: When we use this card, people will read the Bible thought, and learn about the Bible. They will enjoy the picture too!

Choose a card to use right away as a greeting for a neighbor. Ask your child to think of a message, print the message, and deliver the card to the neighbor.

May Day

Celebrate the tradition of May Day flowers by giving some to a neighbor. Cut flowers from your yard (let your preschooler point out which ones) or choose a simple bouquet from a nearby store. Place the flowers in a glass jar or wrap the stem ends in wet paper towels and wrap the bunch with pretty paper. Attach a note that says: *Happy May Day! Love, The Neighbors.*

With your child, sneak to a neighbor's house. Place the flowers on the doorstep, ring the doorbell (or knock), and run and hide in a place where you can watch the reaction of the neighbor. After the neighbor has gone inside the house, say: We surprised and showed our neighbor that we love him!

Porch Tea Party

Materials: warm tea (decaf for your preschooler), milk, sugar, cookies, fancy cups and saucers, spoons, tablecloth, candles or vase of flowers

With your child, decorate a porch table with the tablecloth and flowers or candles. Arrange the pretty cups and saucers. Sit down for a family tea party. Talk about how Jesus loves each family member. Ask your child to think of other people Jesus loves. Say: Jesus tells us to love our neighbors. What is a neighbor?

Suggest that your family invite a neighbor family over for tea on the porch.

Safe House

As you build a relationship with your neighbors, ask permission to have one of the houses (and neighbor) be your emergency safe house.

Teach your older preschooler about being safe in case of fire. Show how to crawl out of the house, feel doors to check if they are hot, use stairs (not elevators), or climb out a window if you have a ladder or are on ground level. Practice each procedure. Plan to meet at your neighbor's house. Teach your preschooler how to walk to the neighbor's house and ask for help if there is any kind of emergency at your house. Say: Our neighbor will be a good helper. That's what neighbors are for, to help each other.

Some important things your child needs to know:
• First and last name
• Home address and phone number
• Parent name
• How to dial 911 on the telephone
• Safe house location

Tip: If you do not have a close neighbor, select a special tree or spot in your yard for a family meeting place in case of emergency.

Holiday Treats

With your child, choose a favorite recipe for cookies, cupcakes, or candy. Gather the ingredients, and make the special treats together. Place several on a paper plate that is wrapped with holiday paper. Cover with plastic wrap, and attach a card that conveys holiday greetings. Include a Bible verse about Jesus' birthday. Let your child top it with a bow. Recognize your neighbors by delivering a plate of home-baked cookies or treats. Say: Merry Christmas! Thank you for being our neighbors.

Invite your neighbors to attend holiday services at your church. Share why you celebrate Christmas.

Holiday Messages

Convey the reason you celebrate Easter, Thanksgiving, and Christmas. Select wrapping paper, greeting cards, and decorations that show your beliefs about Jesus. Choose decorations or cards that express the true meaning of each holiday, not the commercialized meaning. Let your child help look for cards or paper that have pictures of the Nativity, the Resurrection, or nature themes. Say: We can tell our neighbors about Jesus by what we wrap presents in or by what pictures are on our cards.

Welcome Bread

With your preschooler, make homemade bread following a favorite recipe (or buy frozen bread loaves, thaw, and bake). Let your child help add ingredients, knead, punch down, and form the loaves. Enjoy one loaf of bread with your family.

Welcome a new neighbor with the other loaf of fresh bread. Ask your child to help you wrap the cooled bread in plastic wrap and then foil. Let your child draw a picture on a piece of paper. Add your home contact information and an invitation to call if the new neighbor needs help or has a question. Say: A good neighbor welcomes new people. New neighbors don't know anyone that lives around them. Now our new neighbor will know us!

Give the bread to your preschooler to carry. Deliver the bread to the new neighbor and welcome him to the neighborhood.

Neighborhood Yard Sale

Plan a neighborhood yard sale. Customers will flock to a neighborhood sale. Choose a date for the yard sale. Enlist neighborhood preschoolers and children to make and decorate signs. Add balloons to each sign, and post them the morning of the yard sale. Involve your preschooler by allowing her to sort her toys and belongings and put some things in the sale. Price items with stickers (let your child put the stickers on items). Arrange items on tables or racks.

During the sale, let your child help bag purchases or visit with shoppers. Say: Thank you for helping with the yard sale! You worked with your hands, just like the Bible says.

Offer your older preschooler the chance to have a lemonade and cookie stand during the yard sale. Enlist the help of an older child in your family or a neighbor to help with the snack stand. Help make a sign that includes the prices. Help arrange the cookies, lemonade, and supplies on a table. Give your preschooler a money box to put earnings in.

After the yard sale, work as a team to box remaining items and donate them to a chosen charity.

Tip: During the last two hours, offer customers a bag, and let them fill it with anything for a buck—a bag, a buck!

Build a Neighborhood

Dig out the wooden blocks and accessories, paper, markers, and masking tape. Play with your child as you build a neighborhood with the blocks and accessories. Make signs and tape them to houses or stores. Drive toy cars and walk dolls around the neighborhood. Say: A neighborhood is a place that people live and work and go to school. We live in a neighborhood.

Summer Family Play Day

Invite your neighbors to a family play day hosted in your yard (or a local park). Tell everyone to wear clothes that can get wet and messy. Arrange preschooler-friendly activities like:
- Finger painting—acrylic or tempera paint, pieces of cardboard, finger paint
- Shaving cream painting—shaving cream, serving trays or a card table (legs closed and table flat on ground)
- Wading pool—wading pool, water, toy boats, plastic containers for pouring water, towels
- Hula hoops and balls
- Cookie decorating—cookies, butter knives, canned icing, paper plates
- Sprinkler to run through
- Sand tub—sand in plastic tub, scoops, plastic cups
- Rest quilt—quilt in the shade, books about Jesus or church

Ask for help from other parents. Let your preschooler plan favorite games she likes to play. Help her call her friends to come over and play. Invite passersby to join the fun. Tell your child: Neighbors are important. We can tell our neighbors about Jesus. Caution: Provide waterproof sunscreen for families to use.

Family Loss Support

Reach out to neighborhood families that have a loss of a family member. With your preschooler, make a casserole or a dessert. Go with your child to deliver the food. Offer prayer, help, or even babysitting. Be available for talking. Follow up after the funeral when things have settled down. Show neighborly concern and helpfulness. Share similar situations that have happened to you, and how the Lord has helped you through them. Continue to offer help, and make contact with grieving family members. Show your child that neighbors take care of each other when sad things happen. Say: Jesus told us to love each other. Neighbors love each other by helping when sad things happen.

Family Bible Study

Begin a family Bible study at your home. Keep the format simple. Plan a short, family-oriented Bible story, a Bible verse reading, sharing prayer requests, and prayer. Include a prop for the story to engage young listeners in the Bible study. For example, if you tell the story of Noah and the ark, show a toy boat. Prepare a simple snack of cookies or cake, coffee, tea, and milk. Select a night of the week that doesn't interfere with school or church activities.

Invite one of your neighbor families to attend the family Bible study. Include all ages of children in the study. Keep the study short, but include time for discussion and asking questions. Provide paper and pencils for younger children to use to draw pictures about the story. Thank your neighbors for coming to the Bible study. Continue the study each week.

Tip: Ask your child to suggest a favorite Bible story for the study. Your pastor can give ideas of good Bible studies for families.

Laundry Neighbors

Occasionally, wash your clothes at a self-service laundry, even if you have a washer and dryer at home. Take a couple of loads of dirty clothes, your preschooler, and a tub filled with preschool-aged games, puzzles, toys, markers, and paper. Tell your child: We are going to meet new neighbors at the laundry. We can tell our new friends about Jesus, or invite them to come to church with us.

As you wash and dry your laundry, play with your child and the tub of fun activities. Invite other preschoolers or children who are waiting while their parents wash clothes to join your fun. Learn their names and introduce yourself to their parents. Begin to build a relationship with the new people. Find out if they live in your neighborhood, if they go to church or a local school, where they work, and so on.

Find out when the new friends usually do their laundry, and return with your child and the tub of fun activities to visit again. Tell about your church, and invite them to attend with you. Or offer to pray for needs or concerns that have been mentioned during your conversations. Say: I'm so glad that God has brought us together!

Hot Cocoa and Prayers

Ask your preschooler to help you prepare hot cocoa with marshmallows on top (use an ice cube to cool off your child's cup of cocoa). Snuggle as you drink your hot cocoa. Talk about the neighbors you have met. Say a simple prayer that each neighbor will hear about and love Jesus.

Shop in Your Neighborhood

Include your preschooler on shopping trips. Frequent neighborhood businesses. Use the shopping excursions to get to know employees, owners, and other shoppers. Let your child interact with other people and meet future friends! Make yourself and your child friendly, approachable, and helpful. As you get to know people, offer prayers for specific needs, share resources, or tell how God has helped you in similar circumstances. Make relationships with the intention of sharing about God. Tell your preschooler: God wants us to tell others about Him. When we make new friends, we can tell them about God.

Walk the Line

Find a line painted on a sidewalk or empty parking lot. Walk the "balance-beam" line with your child. Hold her hand as she walks along a curb edge or cement parking block. Point out features of your community as you walk. Say: Jesus loves all of the people in our neighborhood. Let's love the people too, just like He does.

Snowman Fun

With your child, visit with neighbors and businesses and ask them to decorate a snowman for their yard or business (and help decorate the neighborhood).

Ask your preschooler to help make your family snowman. Use snow, cardboard, wood, or other creative materials to make a snowman. Add features like eyes, ears, nose, mouth, hair, arms, clothes, and accessories. Help your child make a sign for your snowman to hold. Use markers and heavy cardboard for the sign. Print *Welcome, Friends!* or *God Loves You!* on your sign, and attach it to the snowman.

Take a walking tour of all of the snowmen. Tell your preschooler to choose his favorite. Comment on snowmen designs and thank neighbors and businesses that participated in the snowman fun. Take pictures!

Going to the Zoo!

Take a trip to the zoo with your family. Look at the animals, and notice how they live: alone, in groups, in the water, grassland, caves, and so on. Talk about how each animal lives in the zoo neighborhood. Look for zoo helpers. Say: The zoo neighborhood has helpers. God wants us to be a good neighbor. A good neighbor is a helper!

11

My World

Read More About It: Matthew 9:37–38; 28:19–20; Mark 16:15; Luke 24:46–48; Acts 1:8; 2 Corinthians 2:14–17

Bible Thoughts for Preschoolers

Everything God made was very good (see Gen. 1:31).
God loved us and sent His Son (see 1 John 4:10).

What is my world?

The world is our planet Earth, in its entirety, from people, plants, and animals, to mountains, deserts, plains, rivers, lakes, and oceans. The world is where we live and interact with fellow human beings. From God's viewpoint, the world is where we live and what sustains us (air, food, water). But more importantly, God views all of the people as the highest of His creations in the world. He loves and cares deeply about each individual person. The people are the world.

For your preschooler, his world consists of the people, things, and places immediately surrounding him. He sees the world as those people and things he interacts with on a daily basis. Your child's world consists of his family, his preschool, his church and Sunday School friends, and his neighborhood. Your child views all people as being similar to him.

Preschoolers are in the very beginning processes of learning about the world (the entire world). What he learns about his own little world will transfer to what he learns about the world as a whole. If he learns that the people around him are loving, caring, and helpful, he will believe that all the people in the world are the same. If he grows up learning the value of each person, regardless of skin color, language, culture, or economic status, he will value all people in the world.

Why is the world important?

God made the world and the people that live on it. If He made people and the world, that means both are important to Him. If something is important to God, then we need to pay attention and make the same things important in our lives.

It is important to God that we get along with others in the world. Since God created each individual, and loves each individual, we should love each person (Gen. 1–2). God made each person unique, special, and worthy of the gift of His Son, Jesus Christ. We should learn and teach the value of people. The world is a huge place, but God still commands us to go, tell, and teach about Jesus. Our little corner of the world is where we need to begin.

Our world is important because it is our place of residence. Besides reaching out to the families around us, we need to be good stewards of the place we live. We need to practice and teach how to care for our surroundings. If we do not take care of our world, it will fall into ruin, and will not help sustain us. Everything we have, God gave us. Everything is a gift from God. To honor Him, we must take care of the people and the things that He has given. When we take care of something, we show how important it is.

How can I teach my preschooler about the world?

Preschoolers learn through experiences. They learn by getting out there and doing and seeing things. They learn by reading books and looking at pictures. Preschoolers learn through conversations and by listening to what parents say. Preschoolers learn about the world by living in the world!

Take your child places. Point out things as you go. Walk outside, and look at the people and creations of God. Enjoy the flowers and plants and trees. Visit parks, museums, and zoos. Go to malls where people from different cultural backgrounds shop. Participate in cultural events offered in your community. Cook and taste foods from other countries. Show your child the interest you have in learning about other people and cultures. He will learn the excitement of discovery from you. Embrace diversity in your city, and show your child that each person is unique and loved by God.

Activities

World Learning Area

Materials: globe, children's picture atlas, Bible, world puzzle, world map

Arrange a family world learning area. Place the items on a table. Refer to them often as you talk about things that happen in the world, places you see on television or read about in books, or people you meet. Encourage your child to look at the atlas, work the puzzle, and find places on the map or the globe. Look up the Bible thoughts from this chapter. Say: The Bible tells us that God made everything. He made the entire world, and all the people on the world. He loves everyone!

Note: This is recommended only for kindergarten-age preschoolers.

Ethnic Foods

Take your child out for lunch or dinner to an ethnic food restaurant. Talk about the smells of the food cooking, the sounds (music or people speaking another language), the tastes of the food, and the decorations at the restaurant. Decide which country the foods originated from. Say: God loves all the people in the world. He made each one different and special.

Go home and look on a map or globe for the country that was represented at the restaurant. Look in the atlas to find pictures of people from that country.

Coffee Table Map

Cover a coffee table with a world map. Place toy boats, airplanes, and cars in a basket on the table. Drive the boats on the water parts of the map. Move the cars along the land masses. Fly the airplanes from continents to continents. Point out the place where you live. Say: This is a map. It is a flat picture of the world, but much, much smaller. People live in all of the countries on this map.

Keep the map and toys on the coffee table. Play often with your preschooler, the map, and the toys. Discuss the ways people get from one country to another.

Note: This is recommended only for kindergarten-age preschoolers.

Footprints

Make footprints with your child. Make footprints with boots walking in snow or mud, bare feet walking in sand or mud, or wet feet walking on dry cement. Step in each other's footprints. Tell your child that missionaries walk in many different places around the world, telling others about Jesus. Say: We can tell others about Jesus in the places that we walk.

Lead your child in a short prayer for the people who tell others about Jesus.

Visit Local Cultural Events

Watch the newspaper and television for ads telling about local cultural offerings. Take advantage of cultural fairs, parades, food carnivals, and holiday happenings. Show your child newspaper pictures that feature people from other countries or cultural events. Take your child on an adventure to nearby events. Taste the foods, listen to the music, and look at the art or traditional clothes. Talk with the people and learn about their culture. Show that you appreciate the way that God made each culture unique.

With your child, say a sentence prayer that the people of each cultural group will learn about and love Jesus.

Tip: Some cultural events include Cinco de Mayo (Mexico), Chinese New Year (China), Boxing Day (England), Powwows (Native Americans), and Kwanzaa (Africa).

Go to the Library

The public library is an excellent source of cultural material. Make a weekly date with your child, just the two of you. Go to the library. Allow your child to choose some books and work some of the puzzles in the children's department. Look at music selections, and check out a CD or cassette of cultural music. Find a book about the same country. Take them home. Play the music and look at the pictures in the book. Read the books your child chose. Talk about people that live in different places all over the world.

United States Road Map

Spread a US map on a table. Use a dark colored marker to draw a long road that winds through each of the states. Make a star at one end for the start and a stop sign at the other end for the finish. Give your preschooler a toy car to drive through all of the states. Help her follow the curving road. Show your child where you live. Say: People live in all of the states. We live in

_____.

FYI: Driving a toy car is good training for little muscles and eyes. The same muscles will later be used for writing and reading.

Note: This is recommended only for kindergarten-age preschoolers.

Bible Thought Place Mats

Materials: old maps, construction paper, markers, glue, scissors, self-adhesive plastic, Bible thoughts from this book

Draw outlines of place mats on the maps. Let your preschooler cut along the lines (help younger preschoolers cut). Print Bible thoughts on pieces of construction paper. Let your child trim the excess paper from around each Bible thought. Help him glue a Bible thought in the center of each place mat. Cut pieces of self-adhesive plastic a little larger than the place mats. Carefully peel off the protective backing, and lay place mats front side down onto the sticky side. Cut a straight line into each corner (see sketch), and fold edges over the back. Smooth.

Use the place mats at mealtime. Let your child set the table. Read the Bible thoughts, talk about what each means, and the places represented by the maps. Say: The Bible is for all the people who live in the world.

Note: This is recommended only for kindergarten-age preschoolers.

A Ball Hunt

Go for a ball hunt in your home. With your child, gather as many round ball shapes as you can find. Play with the toy balls. Compare the sizes and purposes of the balls that you find. Say: The world is round, like a ball. God made all of the people that live on our round world.

Adopt a Country

Ask your child to help you choose a country. Learn about the chosen country. Some ways to learn about a country:

- Read about it in reference books, world atlas, or other books.
- Listen to music from the country.
- Look for and prepare a recipe from the country.
- Search the Internet for information.
- Watch for news articles or features on television.
- Attend a local cultural event centered on the country.

Keep the learning fun by making it simple. Your child will be most interested in tasting foods, playing games, hearing music, and seeing clothing from another country. Say: Jesus loves everyone, but not everyone has heard about Jesus. Some people go to other countries to tell about Jesus. We call those people missionaries. We are missionaries where we live. Jesus wants us to pray for missionaries.

Support Your Missionaries

With your child, ask church leaders if your church supports any missionaries. Ask for the names, contact information, and place of service for the missionaries. Contact a missionary. Introduce yourself and your child. Ask for things to pray about and if the missionary and family have any needs. Many missionaries have email letters and prayer chains that you can sign up for.

Pray for the missionary by name with your child. Look on a map to see where the missionary lives. Collect, package, and mail needed items. Say: A missionary is a person who tells about Jesus and serves others.

Shape Game

Make the shape of a circle, a rectangle, and a cross on index cards. Place the cards in an envelope and put it in the car. The next time you are driving somewhere with your child, pull out a card. Show her the card and ask her to name the shape. Help her look for things outside of the car that are the same shape. After a while, switch to a new shape. Say: Our world is in the shape of a circle. The Bible is the shape of a rectangle. Sometimes we can see a cross on a church building. God made people in all sizes, shapes, and colors.

Painting in the Park

Take along the following painting supplies when you visit the park: several 2-by-3-foot pieces of cardboard, clothespins, large sheets of white construction paper, plastic cups, gallon of water, paintbrushes, liquid paint in yogurt cups (with lids), basket or tub to carry supplies

Play at the park with your child. When it's breaktime, sit in the shade and bring out the paint supplies. Use clothespins to clip a piece of paper onto a cardboard easel, open the paints, and let your child paint. Prepare an easel for yourself, and show how to make simple designs, like a heart, a sun, a house, and a cross. Encourage your child to cover the entire paper with paint, not just a tiny corner or the center. Watch for other children that seem interested in painting. Let your child invite them to join the activity. Share about Jesus, and tell each person that Jesus loves him. Give each his painting to take home.

Balloon Toss

Inflate several large blue and green round balloons. Toss the balloons with your preschooler. Try to keep the balloons from touching the ground. Talk about how God made the world to float in space, and orbit around the sun. Say: These balloons are round, just like our world. Our world is covered with green land and blue water.

Note: If balloons pop, they can be a choking hazard for preschoolers.

Prayer Bike Ride

Put on the safety helmets and go for a bike ride with your preschooler. Let your older child ride a tricycle or bike with training wheels. Give your baby or toddler a free ride in a baby bicycle seat. When you stop for rest, a drink, or a bathroom break, say a sentence prayer for people who ride bicycles in big cities. Pray that the bicycle riders will learn about Jesus. Say: Many people around the world ride bicycles to work. God gave us strong legs to make a bicycle (tricycle) work!

Lace World Prayer Reminder

Materials: 4-inch balloon, liquid starch, bowl, blue and green crochet thread, scissors, waxed paper, apron

Let your child pour some of the starch into the bowl. Cut a long piece of each color of thread, and ask her to soak them in the starch. As the thread soaks, inflate the balloon. Say: We are going to make a world prayer reminder. Each time we see this hanging in our house, we can say a prayer that the people in the world hear about Jesus.

Help your child wrap a thread around the balloon, changing directions, and crossing the thread over itself several times. Change colors, and repeat. Stop adding thread when the balloon is half covered, and parts of the balloon are still visible. Cut off the thread, and tuck the end behind another thread. Lay the balloon on the waxed paper to dry. After the balloon is dry, pop the balloon. Throw away balloon pieces. Make a loop with a piece of string, and tie it to the string ball. Hang the world in your home. Say a prayer for all people to hear about Jesus.

Tip: Make several of the lace worlds. Sprinkle on glitter while they are wet. Use as holiday ornaments, or give to friends and family and ask them to pray for the people in the world who do not know Jesus.

Go Fish Card Game

Ask your child to help you make a card game from index cards. Use markers or rubber stamps to make four each of the following: hearts, crosses, churches, Bibles, stars, worlds, and hands.

Mix the cards, and put them in a stack, facedown. Follow the rules for Go Fish. Deal seven cards to each player. Show your child how to hold the cards and ask for a certain card. Tell players that all four of a suit must be found to make a match. After all cards have been matched, look at the pictures. Ask your child to tell what each means and why it is important.

International Dinner

Host an international dinner at your home. With your child, make invitations by cutting pieces of a world map and gluing them onto a piece of folded cardstock. Print the invitation inside the card, including date, time, place, and what to bring. Ask guests to bring a favorite international food and the recipe. Deliver the cards with your child.

Let your child help choose an ethnic food to prepare. Work together to fix the special dish. Ask your child to help decorate your home. Spread a world map on the table, cover it with a clear acrylic tablecloth, and add candles. Place a globe and a Bible near the front door. Supply paper plates, cups, napkins, plastic utensils, juice, and coffee. Play instrumental music.

With your preschooler, welcome guests at the door. Show where to put the food items. After all guests have arrived, let each tell about the food they brought and the country where it originated. Say a prayer, thanking God for a wonderful world, and the delicious variety of foods prepared. Enjoy the food and share recipes.

Stained Glass World

Materials: picture frame glass, taken out of frame; masking tape; watered down white glue; paintbrush; yellow, orange, blue, and green 1-inch squares of tissue paper; permanent marker

Place a piece of masking tape along the edges of the glass. Draw a large circle in the center of the glass. Tell your child to paint inside the circle with glue, and stick blue and green tissue paper squares on the glue. Next, let him paint glue over the rest of the glass, and cover it with red and orange paper. After the glass is dry, carefully pull masking tape off the edge and place it back into the frame (without the backing). Tape the glass to the frame.

Hang the stained glass world in a window. Ask your child to look at the light streaming through the colors. Say: Everything God made is good. He made the world for us to enjoy. Many artists make stained glass pictures of the beautiful things that God has made.

Art Center

Materials: washable desk or table, containers to hold supplies, paper organizer, colored paper, envelopes, stickers, scissors, pens, pencils, markers, crayons, glue sticks, old magazines for cutting, bulletin board, pushpins

Let your preschooler help you set up an art center. Organize art supplies on the desk or table. Fill paper organizer with paper, magazines, and envelopes. Attach the bulletin board over the desk.

Let your child make beautiful works of art and display them on his bulletin board. Say: God loves us, and sent His Son, Jesus. He also made beautiful things for us to enjoy because He loves us.

Encourage your child to make pictures and greeting cards. Send a card to a friend or relative who is ill, or to a missionary who is telling about Jesus in another place.

Caution: Gear art supplies to the age of your child.

Stamp Collecting

Get your child excited to receive the mail! Purchase a notebook or journal and glue sticks. As mail arrives, let your child carefully trim the stamps off of the envelopes. Another way to remove stamps is to soak them in cool water, which loosens the glue. Let her put glue on the back and stick the stamp into her stamp album. Look at the stamp, and decide where it came from. Use a map or globe to locate states or countries featured on the stamps. Say: Each stamp is like a little storybook about a place in the world. It tells about a place and people that God loves.

Say a prayer for the person who sent the mail, and for the people who live where the stamp came from.

Hint: Check the backs of magazines or newspapers for ads to purchase stamps. Some companies have large numbers of stamps for low prices.

Note: This is recommended only for kindergarten-age preschoolers.

World Soaps

Materials: laundry soap flakes, bowl, hand lotion, waxed paper, 8-inch pieces of cord

Let your child dump soap flakes into the bowl. Add a small amount of lotion, and let your child mix the lotion and soap together with his hands. Continue adding lotion until the soap forms a ball. Show how to pinch off a small piece about the size of a plum, and form it into a world shape. Fold a piece of cord in half, and tuck the ends into the ball of soap. Smooth the soap over the cord ends. Place on waxed paper to dry. Repeat with the remainder of the soap.

Use the world soaps for your family. Or attach a Bible thought from this book, and give them out as gifts to people who are important in your child's life. Say: These little soaps are round like the world. Who could we give one to?

Parent Helps and Reproducibles

Bible Thoughts
(Printed in order of use in this book.)

Jesus loves you (see John 15:12).

Love one another (see 1 John 4:7).

God is good to us (see Psalm 73:1).

God gives us things to enjoy (see 1 Tim. 6:17).

Be kind to each other (see Eph. 4:32).

God cares for you (see 1 Peter 5:7).

Jesus prayed (see Matt. 14:23).

Pray for one another (see James 5:16).

Give thanks to the Lord for He is good (see Psalm 107:1).

God loves a cheerful giver (see 2 Cor. 9:7).

Jesus went about doing good (see Acts 10:38).

We work together (see 1 Cor. 3:9).

We are helpers (see 2 Cor. 1:24).

Serve one another (see Gal. 5:13).

A friend loves at all times (see Prov. 17:17).

Jesus said, "You are my friends" (see John 15:14).

I like to go to church (see Psalm 122:1).

Jesus went to church (see Luke 4:16).

Jesus said, "Love one another" (see John 15:17).

Work with your hands (see 1 Thess. 4:11).

Everything God made was very good (see Gen. 1:31).

God loves us and sent his Son (see 1 John 4:10).

Soup Mix Gift Jar
(chap. 5, p. 69)

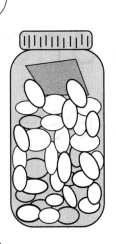

Fill a large soup pan with 4 quarts of water. Bring to a boil and add dried beans and rice. Cover, turn down heat, and simmer for 30 minutes, stirring often. Add water if needed. Add spice packet, stir, and continue cooking until beans are soft, at least 30 minutes.

If desired, top with sour cream or grated cheese. This soup is delicious served with corn bread. Enjoy!

Sample Good Friends Bible Club Plan

(chap. 6, p. 80)

1. **Craft**—Heart collage (10 minutes). Precut heart shapes from red construction paper. Cover the craft area with newspapers. Gather scraps of paper, lace, string, ribbon, buttons, and other craft items. Place in a container. Provide glue. Invite preschoolers to glue craft items onto a heart shape. Say: We love our friends. Jesus loves us.

2. **Song** (5 minutes)—Gather in a circle on the floor. Sing "Jesus Loves Me" and "Jesus Loves the Little Children."

3. **Bible Story** (5 minutes)—Open the Bible to Matthew 19:13–15 and tell the story about Jesus and the little children in your own words. Keep the story short, but let the preschoolers and parents see you looking into the Bible. Say: Thank You, Jesus, for loving the children. Thank You for loving us!

4. **Game** (5–10 minutes)—Play music and give each preschooler a beanbag or rolled up sock to balance on their heads. March and move in a circle around the room while balancing the beanbag. Toss the beanbags into a basket or gently up into the air.

5. **Snack** (10 minutes)—Ahead of time, prepare crackers, butter, and milk. Pray for the snack and socialize while everyone is eating.

Food Drive Flyer
(chap. 5, p. 71)

Food Drive Collection

What:

Where:

When:

Collected food will go to:

Questions? Contact:

Help us help our community!

**Door Hanger
Pattern**

(chap. 6, p. 84)

**Pet Show Ribbon
Pattern**
(chap. 8, p.102)

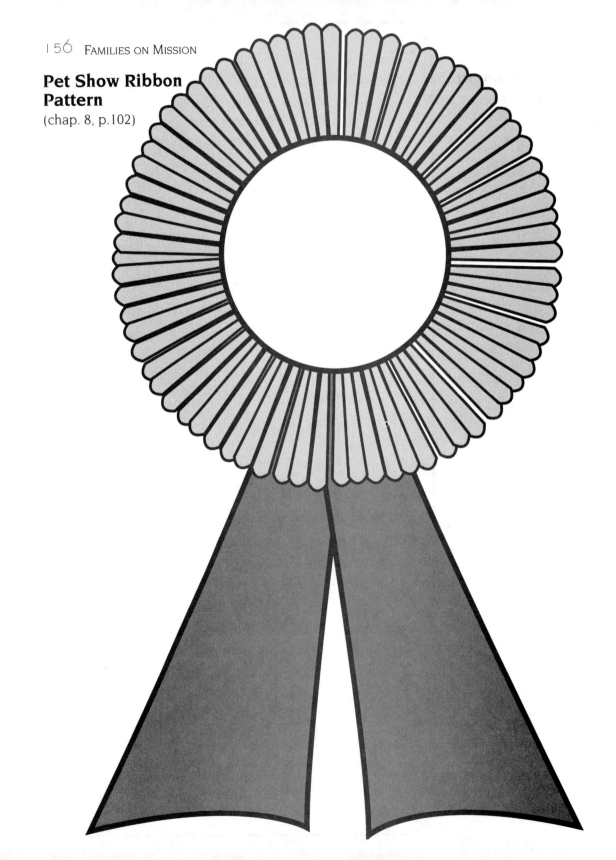

Friendship Stew and a Movie Invitation
(chap. 8, p.108)

Welcome!

You are invited to help make friendship stew
and watch a movie!

Time:

Place:

Date:

Hosted by:

Movie:

Bring one of the following items: cereal rings, pretzels, raisins, chocolate chips.

Questions? Call:

Thank you!

Your purchase of this book and other WMU products supports the mission and ministries of WMU. To find more great resources, visit our online store at www.wmustore.com or talk with one of our friendly customer service representatives at 1-800-968-7301.

WMU®
Discover the Joy of Missions[SM]
www.wmu.com